Silent Whispers

Silent Whispers

SAY

© 2016 by SAY. All rights reserved.

Published by Amorous Ink Publishing Indianapolis, IN 46220

No part of this publication may be reproduced or transmitted in any form or by any means, electronic or mechanical, including photocopy, or any information storage and retrieval system, without permission from the publisher. The only exception is a brief quotation in printed reviews.

Limit of Liability/Disclaimer of Warranty: While the publisher and author have used their best efforts in preparing this book, they make no representations or warranties with respect to the accuracy or completeness of the contents of this book and specifically disclaim any implied warranties of merchantability or facilities for a particular purpose. No warranty may be created or extended by any persons. The advice or strategies herein may not be suitable for your situation. You should consult with a professional where appropriate. Neither the publisher nor author should be liable for any loss of profit or any other incidental damages, including but not limited to special, consequential, or other damages.

This is a work of fiction. Names, characters, businesses, places, events and incidents are either the products of the author's imagination or used in a fictitious manner. Any resemblance to actual persons, living or dead, or actual events is purely coincidental.

ISBN 978-1-943159-03-1
Library of Congress Control Number
2016904329

The publisher would appreciate notification where errors occur so that they may be corrected in subsequent printing and/or editions. Please send comments to the publisher by emailing to biz@leftthought.com

Printed in the United States of America

Silent Whispers

Bringing Awareness, Compassion, and Healing to the SELF

In *Silent Whispers* the reader will learn deeply about self-discovery, and then self-empowerment. I talk about my physical, emotional, and spiritual healing. I share my self-discoveries of deep old programs and patterns which have constantly caused me much pain.

The purpose of *Silent Whispers* is to create an exhilarating opportunity for learning in an unbiased, non-judgmental atmosphere free of barriers, and boundaries, for the reader. As I share my own experiences and bring awareness into my own silent whispers (self-talk) of how I truly feel about myself and the world around me, I open the door for the reader to do the same and reflect onto their life and how they can begin to make connections.

Further, I talk about silencing the mind and clearing the heart of pain to then listen to the higher self. My main philosophy is that we all already have everything we need inside of us to be successful; all we need to do is look within and start believing in ourselves. Then, trusting in ourselves and in the universe to develop certainty that we can handle anything that comes into my life is a key to ones' personal power and self-empowered.

Also, breaking free of a life of negative patterns and programs that are non-serving are important to changing ones' hopeless story. Learning that you are enough and we are powerful beyond measure. By changing my story and my focus we begin to create a better life for ourselves. Freeing ourselves of the past pain and gravitate to living a life filled with integrity, wholeness, kindness and unconditional love for ourselves and others

One of the biggest tools I refer to in *Silent Whispers* is the nonviolent communication. The four components of Nonviolent Communication are Observing without evaluating, Identifying and expressing feelings, Identifying needs, and making requests using positive language.

Silent Whispers reinforces learning to dream, setting positive expectations, living in the present, changing ones' story and connecting to the Earth to all be part of using ones' personal power.

My other interest that motivated me to write *Silent Whispers* are my great passion in personal growth, meta-physics, quantum physics, neuroscience, and all forms of healing (spiritual, physical, and emotional). I have spent 20 years studying and applying these areas to my life. Also, my vision, my purpose, my love in life is to empower myself to live the best life I can, fully in the present, in gratitude, to have faith that all is well really inspired me to write this book.

	Introduction
Chapter 1	Nonviolent Communication

The Self, The story

Chapter 2	Programs
Chapter 3	Patterns
Chapter 4	Discovering

Breaking Free from a Life of Evaluations

Chapter 5	Detoxifying the Mind
Chapter 6	Healing Using the Script
Chapter 7	Healing Using Affirmations / Incantations
Chapter 8	Healing Using Energy Cards
Chapter 9	Healing by Connecting to the Earth

Living a Life through Observations

xi

Chapter 10   Learning to Dream and setting positive expectation

Chapter 11   Being Positive and Living in the Present

FORWARD

Dear Reader,

I want to be known as SAY, which are the initials of my three children names. In order to provide an unbiased platform, I have decided not to disclose my identity. Because most likely I will never meet you, I will not know anything about you either—not your gender, nationality, race, religion, social status, profession—absolutely nothing about you. Yet I want to connect with you at the highest level, the level of our humanity, a commonality that is real and so needs to be appreciated.

My hope is that *Silent Whispers* creates an exhilarating opportunity for learning in an unbiased, non-judgmental atmosphere free of barriers, boundaries, and obstacles. In this book, I will share my own experience as I bring awareness into my own silent whispers (self-talk) to live an empowering life. I will talk about silencing the mind and listening to the heart. My main philosophy is that we all already have everything we need inside of us to be successful; all we need to do is look within and start believing in ourselves. One valuable tool I recommend throughout my book is the Nonviolent Communication Method, which can help us compassionately connect with ourselves and others, building cooperation and trust in our lives.

Writing this book has been a motivational tool for improving my self-esteem, my self-trust, providing self-reflection of my significance and belonging, and discovering self-guidance. I hope you will enjoy reading my discoveries and learning how I have formed connections within my life. I believe all our answers come from within our own awareness of our higher true self. My journey takes me to a new awakening of awareness in my own abilities to co-create the life I desire. There is no judgment and no blame—just awareness of and compassion for the self.

With warm loving healing,

Yours truly,

SAY

INTRODUCTION

There was once a wise person who said when referring to people,

"There is no such thing as GOOD or BAD people, because the GOOD people have bad in them and the BAD have good in them."

How often are people characterized or evaluated as "good" or "bad"? I know I have a tendency to classify people into groups. Sometimes it's so natural that I am not even aware that I am evaluating others. At the same time, I have a tendency to evaluate myself as "good" or "bad"—especially in my self-talk.

Recently my daughter went to sleep unhappy because her needs were not being met, so I evaluated myself as a "bad" parent. About the same time, my son started begging us to help him fix pancakes at 8 p.m. Even though this is not a time we typically eat, let alone eat pancakes, we decided to help him. As a result, he was happy, and therefore I evaluated myself as a "good" parent. Whether my evaluations may seem true to others, they are true for me until I otherwise choose to change my mind.

In the same way, I make many evaluations of myself and others around me throughout the day, because that is what my mind is automatically used to doing. My evaluations become a challenge for me to sort through and work out.

Think about how often the media evaluates people in our society—how common is it for a person who harms others to be evaluated as "bad" or "evil" and for a person who brings benefit and joy to others to be evaluated as "good" or "angelic." This is not to say that harming others is okay or the same as helping others. All I am saying is that I have become aware of how often and how easily people and things are categorized in our lives.

What difference does it make if people evaluate others and themselves? What causes us to make those evaluations in the first place? Is it simply because the mind wants to categorize and break information into manageable pieces? Do the categories identify what is most important? Many times, I notice that my evaluations come from thinking only with my mind, from the preconceived beliefs I hold true about myself and the world. Therefore, my evaluations are influenced by how I listen. I find that most often my evaluations are encouraged by my self-talk, my mind's inner dialogue. This self-talk happens in my mind so spontaneously that often I am not aware of it until I stop and consciously bring awareness to it.

Why does self-talk happen so spontaneously? Here is my theory. Think about how much society is centered on evaluations. From the moment we are brought into the world and measured for weight and length and Apgar scores, we are continually judged by our parents, doctors, schools, peers, and society. As a result, we inherently tend toward evaluation.

Consider, for example, an infant evaluated as "below average" on developmental growth charts as compared with other infants. This categorization may affect how the parents perceive their baby and later, how the child views herself. My spouse and I were very much concerned about our first two children and constantly compared them on developmental charts. Our evaluation of those comparative statistics became the benchmarks for determining our children developmental progress. By the time our third child arrived, we were tired of all the comparisons and evaluations and decided to focus instead on enjoying our three children and accepting them as individuals.

When children start school, however, the evaluations begin again. I remember taking standardized tests every year to evaluate the development of my skills. The higher the scores, the smarter students were considered to be, and then were divided into classes according to those scores. The labels "gifted," "average," or "below average" may empower some students but it deprives most of them of hope. This dis-empowerment can follow them into adulthood. That was my experience. As a student, my reading skills were evaluated as "below average" in elementary school. I went all the way through elementary, middle school, high school, and college having difficulty reading, spelling, and writing. The reading skill label affected how I viewed myself and how far I thought I could go. I felt embarrassed, sad, disappointed, discouraged, and sorry for myself. Even today when I receive a lengthy email, I feel frustrated and want to skim through it.

Evaluations like these, from birth onward, teach us to constantly judge ourselves and others. Because my education was more focused on developing the mind than nurturing the heart, it has been easier for me to live and work from my mind as an adult. Because I was born into a system that encourages evaluating myself and others, it has become second nature to make such judgments. Evaluation is so ingrained in me that it has become a habitual part of how I process information.

Without a doubt, my evaluations of myself and others directly affect how I feel and act. When my daughter went to sleep unhappy, I felt sad, depressed, and withdrawn. I evaluated myself as a bad parent who was unable to meet her needs. As a result, my need as a parent to feel nurturing was not met. When I helped my son make pancakes even though it was not time for a meal, I felt happy, because I satisfied his desire for pancakes and could evaluate myself as a good parent. These are just two examples, but I have noticed that all of my evaluations directly impact my self-esteem and sense of self-worth, which then trigger my self-talk. So recognizing and understanding these evaluations is very important.

Of course, there are some evaluations in life that are necessary. For example, evaluations by doctors in an emergency room are crucial to their patients' health. Laboratory evaluations done by scientists are necessary to find cures for diseases. The types of evaluations I am focused on in this book are the ones that make judgments and create barriers and obstacles in life. In the next chapter, I will discuss Marshall Rosenberg's concept of Nonviolent Communication, an insightful and highly effective method that has helped me become aware of my judgmental evaluations and how they hinder communication. This awareness enables me to tap into my true higher self and become conscious of my self-talk, which helps me avoid judging myself and others.

Later in the book, I discuss how evaluations are a by-product of programs and patterns. Taken as a whole, the Nonviolent Communication Method has helped me bring awareness to the silent whispers of my mind and then to tap into and listen to the silent whispers of my heart, where the true higher self resides. This journey brings understanding to the self. Please join me on an exciting adventure to discover yourself, embrace what is already present within you, and then connect to what your heart truly desires. Love, acceptance, approval, joy, and peace are all possible!

CHAPTER 1: NONVIOLENT COMMUICATION

Nonviolent Communication (NVC) is an effective tool that has helped me tremendously in gaining awareness of my evaluations. I especially recommend Marshall Rosenberg's book *Nonviolent Communication: Language of Life*. It has helped me tap into my higher true self and bring awareness through my observations, feelings and needs. Through many examples and applications, Rosenberg describes a clear communication method that allows us to express ourselves and also hear others with respect and empathy. He states that through NVC our words become conscious responses based on a powerful awareness of what we are observing. We connect with what we are feeling and wanting instead of our automatic reactions. NVC's main goal is to form a compassionate connection with oneself and others to build cooperation and trust in our lives.

In addition to Rosenberg's books, I also encourage you to read NVC materials by Inbal Kashtan, Sura Hart, and Victoria Kindle Hodson. I have used their insights to create the following summary of Nonviolent Communication.

The four components of Nonviolent Communication are:
1. Observing without evaluating

2. Identifying and expressing feelings
3. Identifying needs
4. Making requests using positive language

The first component of NVC separates observation from evaluation. Inbal Kashtan, author of *Parenting From Your Heart* (a booklet of NVC ideas and application), explains that an observation is a description of what is seen or heard without adding interpretations or judgments.

I was used to equating my observations with my evaluations. Many times my evaluations were so habitual and automatic that I didn't even notice I was judging and labeling. Here is what was happening. I made an observation of what was going on and then evaluated it. I felt without my evaluation, the observation would not be complete. For example, if I observed my son arguing with his little sister, I would observe and automatically evaluate the situation by saying, "You're arguing with your little sister. That's mean." The observation is "You're arguing with your little sister" and the evaluation is "That's mean." To avoid the evaluation, Kashtan recommends that when referring to what someone said, quote as much as possible instead of rephrasing.

The second component of NVC is identifying and expressing feelings—our emotions, not our thoughts. At first I thought this was an obvious step. To my surprise, I found that many times when communicating, I interpreted my thoughts to be my feelings. For example, when I say, "I feel like this is important," I am expressing a thought, not a feeling. Therefore, NVC recommends against beginning a statement with "I feel that" or "I feel like" because the next words will be thoughts, not emotions. Also, avoid using phrases such as, "I feel misunderstood," "I feel manipulated," or "I feel uncomfortable," because, according to Rosenberg, these words are assessments of the other person's behavior instead of expressions of our own feelings. Rather, the correct words that could express our feelings in those cases could be "I feel annoyed" or "I feel frustrated."

One of the most helpful points I learned from Nonviolent Communication was to build a vocabulary of my feelings, which enables me to clearly express them. Here are some NVC vocabulary words that express feelings when needs are being met:

Absorbed, adventurous, affectionate, alert, alive, amazed, appreciative, comfortable, concerned, confident, contented, curious, dazzled, delighted, eager, ecstatic, encouraged, energetic, enthusiastic, fascinated, free, friendly, fulfilled, glad, grateful, happy, helpful, hopeful, inspired, involved, loving, joyous, moved, optimistic, pleased, proud, refreshed, relaxed, relieved, satisfied, secure, sensitive, surprised, tender, thankful, thrilled, touched, warm, wonderful

Here are some NVC vocabulary words that express feelings when needs are not being met:
Angry, annoyed, anxious, ashamed, bitter, bored, brokenhearted, cold, concerned, confused, depressed, disappointed, discouraged, disgusted, dull, embarrassed, exhausted, frightened, frustrated, gloomy, guilty, heavy, helpless, hesitant, horrified, hurt, impatient, jealous, lazy, lonely, mad, mean, miserable, nervous, overwhelmed, panicky, passive, puzzled, resentful, sad, scared, sensitive, shocked, sorry, suspicious, tried, uncomfortable, unhappy, withdrawn, worried.

At times, expressing our feelings may seem uncomfortable or scary, because they express our vulnerability. However, the more I practice expressing my feelings through clear and honest communication, the more I get my needs met. (Please refer to chapter 4 of *Nonviolent Communication* by Marshall Rosenberg for an in-depth explanation.)

The third NVC component is connecting our feelings with our needs. "I feel _____ because I need _____." In this method, identifying and then expressing our needs is the goal. Like feelings, many of our needs are universal, ongoing, and not dependent on the actions of others. I found it challenging to identify my needs at times. For example, when I make an evaluation of someone, I alienate myself from my own needs. My energy and focus is spent on evaluation, which leads to a judgment, and I get further away from what I really want. I have experienced this several times when my spouse and I get into an argument. When the evaluation and criticism begins, it seems like we are stuck in an evaluation spiral and cannot stop. What's important to us (our needs) gets lost in the spiral. Instead, when we focus on what we are feeling and needing, we are better able to focus on what is important to us. An example of using NVC to express feelings and needs is, "I feel annoyed because I need more support," rather than "I feel annoyed because you were late." Some common human needs discussed by Sura Hart and Victoria Kindle Hodson in *Respectful Parents, Respectful Kids* are as follows:

Fun, play, learning, choices

Relationship with our self: Achievement, acknowledgment, authenticity, challenges, clarity, competence, creativity, integrity, knowing our gifts and talents, meaning, privacy, self-development, self-expression, self-worth

Relationship with others: Appreciation, belonging, sharing life's joys and sorrows, closeness, community, consideration, emotional safety, empathy, honesty,

interdependence, kindness, love, power-with reassurance, respect, sharing gifts and talents, support, to matter to someone, trust, understanding, warmth
Relationship with the world: Beauty, contact with nature, harmony, inspiration, order, peace, security
Physical nurturing: Air, water, food, shelter, protection, rest, sexual expression, exercise, touch.

The fourth component of NVC is making a request using positive language. Here we focus on what we want instead of what we don't want. Kashtan says that "by definition, making requests implies that we are willing to hear 'no' and view it as an opportunity for further dialogue." The words "would you be willing to" were recommended to start a request. For example, if I say to my son, "Would you be willing to mop the kitchen?" and he says no, I accept his answer and look at it as a further opportunity for conversation and connection.

Empathy is also an important concept of NVC, where we aim to respectfully understand others by guessing their feelings and needs rather than "being right" or "getting what we want." In another words, when empathizing we reflect back or paraphrase what we heard. Rosenberg describes empathy as "emptying our mind and listening with our whole being."

The most difficult part of empathy for me is to stay with it and allow others the opportunity to fully express themselves before I turn my attention to my own needs and wants. Often, as I am empathizing, I have a desire to find a solution, make a request, give advice, or reassure. Hart and Hodson give a list of common non-empathetic responses that are unlikely to result in having our needs met at times when connection is the goal:

Advising: I think you should. . .

Commiserating: That's terrible. She had no right to do that to you.
Consoling: Everything's going to be okay.
Correcting: It's not really that hard.
Educating: You can learn from this.
Explaining: I didn't want to do it this way, but . . .
Evaluating: If you hadn't been so careless . . .
Fixing: What will help you is to . . .
Interrogating: What are you feeling? When did you start feeling this way?
One-upping: You should hear what happened to me . . .

Shutting down: Don't worry. It will go away.
Story-telling: Your story reminds me of the time . . .
Sympathizing: You poor thing.

This is not to say that any of these behaviors are wrong, because sometimes sympathy or advice, etc., is what's requested. Therefore, it is important to recognize when our response is automatic or deliberate versus when it is consistent with what's requested.

Rosenberg further states in *Nonviolent Communication*: "We need empathy to give empathy. When we sense ourselves being defensive or unable to empathize, we need to (1) stop, breathe, give ourselves empathy; (2) scream nonviolently; or (3) take time out." Therefore, self-empathy is just as important as giving empathy to others. Self-empathy can be done by listening to our self-talk to determine what we are feeling and needing. For example, if my self-talk is: "I am stressed out and tired!" what I really need is to rest.

I also like the way Kashtan talks about self-empathy in *Parenting from the Heart*:

> Self-empathy can give us 'breathing room' for facing life, much like a meditation practice. While it may not solve every problem, it may

actually help us accept the times when we cannot find a 'fix.' Through self-empathy, we can provide for ourselves some very powerful resources: connection and nurturing for ourselves; focus on what matters most to us; access to creative problem-solving; space to grow and deepen our skills; and confidence that we will act more often in ways that bring us joy and satisfaction.

The philosopher J. Krishnamutri said, "To observe without evaluation is the highest form of human intelligence." This is the greatest challenge of applying the NVC method. When you have spent your whole life evaluating and being evaluated, it naturally takes time to consciously stop and reverse this behavior.

I have found that when I observe without evaluation, I am much happier. Now that I have become familiar with the NVC method, I notice when I am judging or blaming with perceived stereotypes in my mind, which usually causes me some pain and suffering. In the chapters to come, I will describe how, as I start to observe, I first listen and quiet my mind so that I can hear the silent whispers of my heart.

THE SELF – THE STORY

I believe our answers come from within us. It's just a matter of self-discovery and then practicing with tools such as NVC. After learning NVC, I realized the negative impact of my evaluations and am eager to practice and apply NVC in my life. My main struggle is moving from evaluating to observing. As a result, I feel frustrated, because I want to stop evaluating and create connection, understanding, and consideration for myself and for others. But my evaluating happens so automatically and naturally, it is as if I cannot stop. When I evaluate, I am left playing victim, where the blame goes to someone else. Also, I remember that I am brought into a world surrounded with ongoing evaluations and judgments from my caretakers and surroundings, which could have been inherited. As a result, I feel as if my mind is already pre-wired with all these evaluations. For example, evaluations as simple as *it's a boring, rainy day* can turn every rainy day into a boring one. Whereas *it's a great day* can turn any day to a bright one.

My evaluations affected me to the point where they had become a part of my character and me. Therefore, I wanted to break free of judgmental evaluations and start observing in my life. My journey continued as I searched. The next chapter is what I discovered.

CHAPTER 2: PROGRAMS

Evaluations come from our pre-wired programs. Programs are beliefs, stories, and thoughts—silent whispers of the mind—that we have made up about ourselves and the world. These pre-wired beliefs and judgments are the result of a certain event or events. These events may be connected to loved ones, other people, news media, and/or to information on the Internet. Our programs become part of our self-talk and can affect how we view the world and ourselves on an ongoing basis.

Many programs are stored at the subconscious level but can be brought to consciousness. Programs can have an adverse effect on our health and may trigger emotions such as depression, tension, low self-esteem, anger, or resentment.

My first exposure to my own programs was through the Personal Success Institute Basic Seminar, which I took several years ago. The course was about self-exploration of programs in the conscious and subconscious mind. It was interesting how my programs were similar to those of the rest of other participants in the class. Here are examples of a program exercise shared by participants in class.

- At age 11, a classmate says, "I don't want to be your friend." The belief is created that "I am not fun and I am not special."

- At age 5, her parents relocated to the U.S. without her. The belief is created that "I am not worthy."

- At age 4, a little boy cries and doesn't receive any comfort. The belief is created that "I am not lovable."

- A teacher says to a class of 10-year-old's, "Mike is great in math." Some students in the class create a belief that "I am not smart."

The program exercise revealed that almost all the participants were deeply hurt by their own belief systems. They wanted acceptance, approval, affection, and love but did not feel deserving.

According to the PSI Basic Seminar:

- By ages 0-4 years, 50% of our beliefs are formed.

- By ages 4-8 years, another 30 % of our beliefs are formed.

- By ages 8-18 years, another 15% of our beliefs are formed.

- By age 18, 95% of our programs are formed.

Wow, to enter adulthood with 95% of beliefs and judgments formed is an astronomical amount! Almost all of the pre-wiring of how we think and what our self-talk says is already formulated before reaching adulthood. This programming then can be held in any level of our conscious or subconscious mind. What a way to start adulthood, with a pre-wired mind ready to evaluate and judge the self and the world. Programs are the leading cause of depression and misery! Karol K. Truman, author of *Feelings Buried Alive Never Die*, mentions in her book that most people "don't love themselves, don't accept themselves, don't trust themselves, don't like themselves." These are all common programs (beliefs) that are shared, yet each person has their own experiences and events.

I want to share three of my deep programs, which I discovered at the PSI seminar. At age 5, I met my father for the first time in New York City. He decided to take me to work the next day so he could spend the day with me. We lived in Brooklyn and he worked in Manhattan. After spending the entire day with my father, whom I had just met the day before, we left to go back home by train. I was exhausted from the long day and by having to walk to the station and wait for the train. I am sure it was a long day for my father as well. When we finally got on, I was even more exhausted to find that the train was packed and there was no room to sit. I started to cry, because I was so tired, my feet were aching, and I had to remain standing. My father stood quietly by me the entire train ride. I wanted him to hug and comfort me, but maybe he was tired of spending the entire day with a 5-year-old whom he had just met. I remember a woman sitting across from us, smiling; it seemed as if she were trying to empathize with her smile and comfort me. Unfortunately, her smile was not enough. I needed my father's love at that moment. As a result, I formed a belief that "I am not lovable."

I developed another program when I was 16 years old. It was a hot summer day in upstate New York, and I was playing tennis with my best friend in gym class. My friend missed hitting the ball a couple of times and I started to laugh. My friend got very upset and responded to me with, "I don't want to hang out with you anymore. All the rest of my friends ask me why I hang out with you. So after today, stop following me around." At first I thought my friend was joking with me, but much to my dismay, my friend was serious. As a result, we stopped playing tennis immediately and went our separate ways. From that day on throughout high school, not only did I lose my best friend, but also I was unable to make new friends and did not have anyone else to hang around with in school. I remember hating any free times, such as morning homeroom and lunch, because I had no one to talk with. I saw other students hanging around their lockers with friends. I didn't have any friends, so every day I would open my locker and pretend to be cleaning it. Or I would sit in the classroom and open a book and pretend to be reading it, even though I hated reading because I was a very slow reader. From this painful experience of not having friends and not having anyone to hang around with, I formed a belief that "I am not a fun person." From that point on it was very difficult for me to make friends. Even in my college years, I did not have many friends my age.

In my twenties, I started working for a company in a job that I did not enjoy at all. In fact, I hated it. I stayed there for almost nine years because I had to work to pay my bills. Because I didn't finish my bachelor's degree, I thought I had no other choice and was stuck working at a job I hated. As a result, I formed a program that said, "I have no choice." Basically, I started my adulthood with these programs, that I was a person who was not loved, not fun, and had no choice in life. What a way to start off adulthood! I was absolutely miserable in my life. I had so much pain and suffering from my own beliefs, my own programs, but since I felt I had no choice I remained silent. How could I expect anything else with such low self-esteem? I will share more about my programs in the next chapter. Now I will attempt to explain patterns.

CHAPTER 3: PATTERNS

Besides programs, I find patterns are also important in figuring out how to move from evaluation to observation. Patterns are the behavior we choose to do over and over again, so naturally we don't even think about them. The patterns are so automatic that it's almost as if we go into an autopilot mode and are not even conscious of other choices.

For example, learning to drive a car is a common pattern that most of us form. Remember when you learned to drive? At first it may have been nerve-racking and confusing, but after a couple of months or years it became a pretty easy and comfortable task. When you drive today, it requires less thought and focus than when you first learned to drive. The obvious reason is that you have mastered this behavioral pattern by doing it over and over again. Have you ever experienced driving from work or the grocery store and when you get home you did not know how you got there? You cannot recall specific points of driving, because it was done so automatically, as if the car were driving on its own. You may feel as if your mind had no part in the process of driving home. Sounds pretty dangerous! How many times has something like that happened?

How about when you learned to ride a bicycle? Remember how challenging and difficult it was to balance and pedal at the same time? I remember constantly looking down at my feet pedaling and being completely focused on balancing my bicycle. If my focused shifted so did my bicycle—down to the ground. Slowly but surely I gained so much confidence that I no longer needed to pay much attention on balancing and pedaling.

Like driving a car and riding a bicycle, we have developed other patterns in our lives that our mind automatically takes care of without much thought or action on our part. Imagine on a bigger scale how we are living out our patterns.

Patterns are also learned from our family, our environment, our community, and our society. In fact, our first patterns are developed in the womb, even before we enter this world. At the same time, we also may have inherited some generational patterns from our ancestors. This may be why people in a family all seem to behave in a very similar way.

Once, I met a woman who shared that the love she received from her partner never felt enough. She always desired to be loved and nurtured more. She always felt a lack of receiving love from her partner. Later she learned that her father left her mother when she was pregnant with her. When she was in the womb, her mother was alone and longed to be loved. As a result, the desire to be dearly loved was transferred to her, and she inherited her mother's emotional distress pattern.

Other times, we may choose to pick up some conversational patterns from our parents or another influential people in our life. We choose to make someone else's beliefs part of our own patterns in order to take their side or because we view them to be right, successful, and/or powerful. People may live their entire lives using someone else's conversational patterns, living according to someone else's beliefs and accepting their pain, and never even know it.

A close friend shared that he had taken on his father's conversational patterns about his mother and women in general. His parents were separated. At the time, he looked up to his father as a powerful male figure. For survival purposes he decided to side with his father. His father's failed relationship with his mother and experiences with other women resulted in his father having dogmatic views. As a male, my friend subconsciously decided to side with his father and take on his painful conversational pattern and negative baggage concerning women. Consequently, this conversational pattern greatly hindered his relationship with his mother and other women as well. For a long time he blamed his mother and women for his problems in life. As a result, he had a hard time being nice to his mother and a difficult time committing to and staying in a long-term relationship with a woman.

Other patterns can be picked up from society. For example, in most societies boys are raised to think that "real men don't cry." This belief can take so much away from a young boy. Many times boys are made fun of when they express their feelings by crying. Recently we invited a couple of family friends for dinner at our house. It was a nice summer day, so we took our food outside to eat. My youngest son was playing and running around the yard. When he fell, one of the guests told him, "You're okay, you're a tough guy." Are boys focused to be tough from the beginning? As a result, do they have a difficult time expressing their feelings as men, because they develop a pattern of being tough and macho?

All of these patterns—whether picked up from family, friends, or society—form the personality. A person may live most of his or her life on autopilot, operating from behavioral patterns without conscious awareness of them.

Connections Between Programs and Patterns

Sometimes it's our ingrained programs that cause us to develop behavioral patterns. It's a vicious cycle, where we may sabotage ourselves to make our core program beliefs come true.

I can see the connection between my own programs and patterns and the possible self-sabotaging behavior that exists in my life. For example, many times I feel I am not worthy of love. The cause of this program, *I am not lovable*, creates a behavioral pattern of withdrawing from the situation or person. Therefore, when I think I am receiving too much love, I feel embarrassed and uncomfortable, and then withdraw. My marriage feels the effects of this program and behavioral pattern. The more and more aware I become of this connection between my programs and behavioral patterns, the better I am able to identify it. For example, when I am withdrawing from a person or situation, I can notice the feelings of dismay, the "I am not lovable" that lead to it. At times I have a hard time accepting my partner's love. When my partner praises me a lot, whether it's for my good looks or a wise decision I have made, I have a hard time hearing the praise and many times my reaction is an automatic behavioral pattern where I change the subject to something else.

Another program is *I am not fun*. This program causes me to think that my life is boring, that I am a boring person and have nothing interesting to contribute to society. As a result, for many years, anytime I met someone my age, my behavioral pattern was to escape, because I was not interested in carrying on a conversation. I thought I had nothing to contribute. I felt uncomfortable and nervous. My underarms were sweaty. My programs assured me that other people couldn't possibly like me or want to be my friend. The results of this program and the behavioral patterns triggered are that I don't have many friends, and those I do have are usually 10 to 20 years older than I am. I enjoy and feel safe connecting with people on an intellectual level where there will be less risk of being thought of as fun.

A third program is *I do not have any choice*. This program creates the behavioral pattern of feeling depressed and again encourages me not to participate in and contribute to life. The result of this program is resentment. I compare myself to others and notice that everyone else has the opportunity to choose, while I am the only one who doesn't have that privilege. As I compare my life with others, I think my life is not fair. I am a failure. Sometimes, I withdraw from many activities, because I fear that I don't even have the right to choose them. This program and the behavioral pattern allowed me to stay in one miserable job for about nine years. I believed I did not even have the choice to look for something else or to go back to school to finish my degree. I thought I was stuck in that position for the rest of my life, a very dis-empowering feeling. I behaved as though I was powerless to do anything about it.

CHAPTER 4: DISCOVERING PATTERNS AND PROGRAMS

Discovering Patterns

How do we figure out what patterns and programs we are living? Which conversation patterns did we take from someone else and make our own?

First, take three weeks to just be an observer of your behavior, your patterns. Be as objective as possible and make no judgment about your behavior. You will begin to see your patterns. Notice what you are feeling and what you are telling yourself in the silent whispers of your mind. The result of the two will be your behavior. It is important to be gentle with yourself and what you discover. You may observe that you are constantly evaluating and categorizing things. I did that, too, and then I was grouping my behaviors as good or bad. Try to set those labels aside and just be an observer without judgments. Observe your patterns and find the needs and feelings that are not satisfied in order to better understand yourself.

To make it easier on myself for those three weeks, I kept reminding myself to observe from the perspective that all my behavior is simply what I have picked up along the years, and now I am living that behavior out. This perspective helped me to be gentle with myself as I was observing my behavior and discovering new things about myself.

Similar emotional feelings and needs triggered the same behavioral patterns. I also noticed how very automatic my behavior was. For example, when I observed that I felt someone was rude to me, I felt not important or not special, and my pattern was to respond with defensive behavior. This pattern was triggered from feelings of hurt and my need to be respected. My defensive behavior was a means for me to prove to myself that I was important and special. Other times, I simply withdrew because I felt discouraged or dis-empowered. One time a friend invited me to join a club, and I observed that I immediately responded, "I can't." I tried to make excuses to justify why I could not participate, with reasons involving my spouse, my kids, my lack of time, and so on. I hid behind my excuses, although in actuality I was living out of my automatic behavioral pattern of withdrawing from situations where I had to make a choice.

Over and over, I noticed that the same feelings and needs triggered the same automatic responses. After the three weeks, I had a good idea of some of my dominant behavioral patterns. It was interesting to observe further and notice if any of those patterns were someone else's conversations that I picked up and then made mine.

In fact, I had picked up some conversation patterns from my mother and father. I was amazed how silently and proficiently I inherited my parents' conversation patterns. My father was religious speaker and my mother was very spiritual and humble person.

The conversation pattern I picked up from my father is speaking confidently. I am easily able to carry on a conversation with great confidence, even when I do not have much knowledge of the subject matter.

The conversation pattern I picked up from my mother is humility. When I receive a compliment, I quietly begin to downplay my role or achievement for fear I won't be humble. Many times people who have paid me a compliment say, "Can you please just say thank you!" I don't even realize that I haven't said thank you, because my humbling behavior is so automatic. One day when my oldest son was about 4 years old, he gave me a great compliment. He told me, "You could have been a prophet." I smiled at him, and responded with my automatic humbling behavior. I said to him, "No, I couldn't have been a prophet. They were all better human beings and they were all chosen by God." Interestingly, my son now is 15 years old and he continues to tell me "your love and compassionate for humanity is the same as the prophets were." I look at him and smile.

For me, discovering my behavioral patterns has been like finding a missing piece of the puzzle of myself and what makes me tick. As I bring awareness to my behavioral patterns, they help me to understand my needs and feelings and then accept myself.

Discovering Programs

Identifying my patterns has also helped me in figuring out my programs—the reasons I do things. If you choose to discover your own patterns and programs, you will find how they are directly connected and intertwined with each other. For the most part, programs become the foundation and the by-laws from which the silent whispers of the mind (the self-talk) are generated. Programs become our permanent beliefs.

Completing the PSI Basic Seminar greatly helped me in identifying some of my deepest programs.

Discovering those programs was easier than I thought. Here is how it works: I think back to a situation when I was humiliated, insulted, or deeply hurt, and there I will find a program (a permanent belief) that I developed as a result. The two programs I discovered at the seminar were *I am not lovable* and *I am not fun*.

You may make your own connections. Think back to an unpleasant time and the beliefs that were formed as a result. The three questions I ask myself to help me in discovering my programs are:

1. What is it I am feeling?
2. What is it that I think I am not getting?
3. What is it that I am needing?

Or I observe my behavioral pattern and make a connection to the existing program it supports. For example, I notice that when someone is rude to me, my pattern is to respond with defensive behavior. This defensive behavioral pattern is triggered from an existing program. I ask myself the three questions:

1. What is it I am feeling? I feel hurt and angry.
2. What is it that I am not getting? I am not being considered.

3. What is it that I am needing? I need to be respected.

My answers tell me that the program associated with these hurt and angry feelings is *I am not worthy. I am not important enough to be respected and that's why I am mistreated.* I remember a situation when I was a child, where I was constantly scolded. That constant scolding fostered the programs *I am not worthy* and *I am not important*. Today, when someone talks to me in a scolding tone, my programs are reaffirmed. The effects of these programs are carried on, even to the extent that when my children argue or fight with each other, I take it personally. I get upset and start screaming back at them. I fear a lack of love and respect coming from them. I feel I am not worthy of their love, respect, and cooperation. Therefore, I respond with angry words.

It seems to me that my programs result in more programs—a continuing cycle of depressing thoughts that generate more depressing thoughts. For example, the programs *I am not lovable, I am not fun*, and *I am not worthy* resulted in a new program, *I can't have everything I want*.

However, the unique thing about programs is that because they are beliefs that we create about ourselves and the world, we can change them at any time. For as long as we hold a program or a belief to be true, the Law of Attraction ("like attracts like") will continue to create situations in our lives to affirm our programs. Understanding this paradigm is important. Programs involve self-sabotage and are self-destructive. We meet our programs in a revolving door where thoughts become reality.

Discovering programs and patterns was a very big step for me! It helped me to understand why I felt and behaved the way I did in life.

Discovering Through the Obvious Self

Learning about the obvious self has helped me better understand my programs and patterns. The obvious self is when a person operates from habitual behavior and listens to the silent whispers of his or her mind. I like to call this place a habitual comfort zone. The obvious self is not a negative place to be at all. In fact, it's simply where the mind (brain) goes into an autopilot response mode. Years of practice of the same habitual behavior helps form a person's personality and character. Whether the habits are known or unknown to us, or whether they seem like choices or may seem like no choice at all, they are accessed instantly by the obvious self.

Recognizing where I am today with my obvious self helps me to see which patterns and programs exist in my life. My habitual behavior becomes my patterns. The habitual beliefs I hold to be true, the autopilot thoughts, my silent whispers of the mind that I think over and over, are my **programs**. These patterns and programs then become barriers and obstacles that block me from accessing my true feelings and needs.

Where is my obvious self right now? One of the easiest ways I figure that out is to listen to my self-talk or silent whispers. At first it was difficult for me to hear my inner dialogue, but with practice, it got easier.

If you think about it, we communicate to ourselves every moment of our lives through our thoughts. Whenever our thoughts are negative, stressful, worrisome or self-critical, they usually become part of our self-talk. As I become more conscious of my thoughts I begin to hear my self-talk and how it is a big part of me.

Only we can hear our own self-talk. Psychologists estimate that about 72% of all self-talk is self-critical or negative. Try to picture how life is bombarded with patterns and programs playing out in our minds over and over again, non-stop. Many times I notice that my self-talk is filled with evaluations, which make me feel like I am in a battle zone, having a silent war in my mind. Often, my self-talk sounds like: "Oh, I'm getting old, I'm losing my hair, I look fat, I look ugly, I'm stupid, I never understand anything, I will never be good enough, and I'm never going to be perfect." My self-talk, my silent whispers, seem to be so embedded in my mind that they then support and nurture my patterns and program to the point that my responses become automatic, and then I don't need much initiation from the outside to continue it, just affirmation.

Another way I listen to my silent whispers is to observe the way I deal with other people as a paradigm. If I am critical and judgmental of others, then I notice my self-talk is critical and judgmental. If I am compassionate and kind with others, then I notice my self-talk is compassionate and kind. For example, when my daughter comes home from school with a list of complaints, my responses depend on how I feel and what my self-talk is like.

When I am feeling positive, my self-talk is positive. I am able to listen to her feelings and needs without judgment.

There are times, of course, when I am not true to my self-talk and I do not communicate what I feel. I call this faking or acting. I put on a smile and behave positively when I am really miserable and my self-talk is self-critical, self-abusive, and destructive. No one can hear my inner dialogue, but I believe whatever is in my heart eventually appears on my tongue one way or another and the acting gets exposed. The way I treat others is the way I treat myself.

It scares me sometimes how closely the two are connected. Recently, a person close to me mentioned his concern that I was writing this book. Todd (not his real name) said to me, "What are you thinking? There are so many people who write books and get nowhere. You can't be seriously thinking of making money writing, because there are so many people writing—people more educated than you and they get nowhere. I'm telling you, your book will be nothing. You need to start watching television and see what's going on in the real world, because you don't know what's going on out there. People with master's degrees are jobless. People are losing their homes. Wake up and do something!"

I was baffled. First, I felt as if my innermost fears were being rolled up in a ball and thrown at me all at once. Then, I thought maybe this was simply Todd expressing his own inner dialogue, self-talk of his own fears and limits. Therefore, I decided not to make this conversation about myself but to focus on Todd's needs and feelings instead. But my patterns and programs were too overpowering. I became disappointed and angry and withdrew from the conversation. I felt worthless. I felt as if someone had driven over me several times and I now was feeling the aftershock of the pain. I wanted to curl up and die. I felt so sad and wanted to run to an empty room and just cry until I could feel no more pain or had no more tears left.

How could someone else treat me and see me the way I saw myself? How could I treat myself like that? Later, I thought back to the conversation and decided to apply the nonviolent communication strategies. How could my experience have been different? What really were my needs and Todd's needs? My biggest need was for support and encouragement; perhaps Todd's need was to be heard because he was concerned about my future. I re-enacted the whole conversation in my head (which seemed less intimidating than at first), turning Todd's statements into questions and acknowledgments, and listening with empathy. I noticed that my self-talk in the original conversation had started off positive but became negative, because I chose to evaluate Todd's message as negative—that I was not worthy.

The more I became aware of my patterns and programs through my obvious self and self-talk, the more I became aware of the importance that I break free of them. There are two important factors to consider in order to break free from any patterns or programs. The first is acceptance of myself the way I am. The second is to have hope that all will be well. Accepting myself means to observe (receive) my patterns and programs without judging and blaming myself for my obvious self. When I accept myself without any judgment and blame, I nurture self-love and self-understanding of my obvious self.

In her book *Feelings Buried Alive Never Die*, Karol K. Truman recommends that you "give yourself permission—allow yourself to feel whatever feelings you may feel. These feelings are much easier to change if you accept and own them rather than deny them and pretend they don't exist."

Developing a vocabulary for my feelings and needs is also very helpful. I often refer to the feeling and needs from the NVC strategies in chapter 1. I know a man who carries a fold-able business card with feelings and needs on it to refer to throughout his day. Even in an office meeting he can take out his card to stop and reflect on his feelings and needs. I try to carry an index card with me with my most common feelings and needs, so that I can refer to throughout the week. It gives me a sense of security as I go about my day to have that list readily accessible.

I like to think of myself as the co-creator of my life, choosing my own destiny and at the same time having a higher power that is watching over and protecting me. Whatever your religious or spiritual philosophy, you can apply the NVC strategies in your life to help bring hope. I personally enjoy taking time to read, pray, be still, and present in my life for clear openings and growth.

I remember when I was working in a miserable job where I thought I had no other choice. I remember praying each day to find out what my purpose in life was. When I lost my job, I was stressed out at first and didn't know what to do. Eventually I decided to go back to school and finish my bachelor's degree. Looking back on it, I think that losing my job was a sign that my higher power was watching over me and helping move me in the direction of my innermost desires, my self-conscious level of my higher true self.

Discovering Through the Higher True Self

The higher true self is difficult to describe in words. Understanding it with the heart helps it become clear so that no explanation is needed. Nevertheless, I will attempt to describe the higher true self to the best of my understanding. I like to think of the higher self as the inner wisdom—a spark that we are all born with. It is free of any desire to judge, to compete, or to diagnose others. For as long as we live, this spark exists within us. The choice is ours how often we choose to access our spark.

One of the ways we tap into this spark is to listen to our silent whispers of the heart. As a result, I believe that the answers of our higher true self then come from within us.

Acting from the higher self is as natural as smiling whenever you see a baby. It's the feeling you get when someone asks you to donate to a needy cause, and you reach into your pocket and give what you have. For example, last winter, at a place where my children study after school, I saw that there was an organization collecting winter coats for the homeless. We went home and as a family pulled out all our extra coats and donated them. We were acting from the higher self.

What helps me greatly in tapping into my higher self is to be honest with myself, and with my emotions and needs, and then try to accept myself. From the PSI seminar, I learned that there are only two true emotions, love and fear, and everything is a branch of these two root emotions. Fear is generated from the mind and love is generated from the heart. Fear is a learned behavior. Love is a natural behavior that already exists in the heart. In the higher self, the heart is filled with unconditional love and compassion. Some examples of love emotions are love, confidence, trust, happiness, enthusiasm, kindness, and compassion. Some examples of fear emotions are anger, fear, irritation, jealousy, depression, sadness, envy, hate, guilt, resentment, rejection, and doubt.

Some may like to associate this spark or higher self with a divine source. Please make the connection that is most agreeable with your own beliefs or understanding. In fact, I believe self-consciously that there is an authentic desire to be connected to and navigate from our spark, heart, and the higher true self. Perhaps you will find a different interpretation. For me what is important to me is part of me. What is truly important to you is part of you, too. Our truth is our reality. Our truth is our identity. Becoming aware and honest with ourselves will help us connect with our higher self. Here are some questions that helped bring clarity to me regarding what is important.

Who am I?

Where am I from?

Where am I going?

Is there a purpose to my life?

These can be pretty deep questions. Religious beliefs or intellectual understanding often become the foundation for these types of questions, which is great! To me, religion is a very personal and dear subject. Being raised by a clergyman father and a mother who was very spiritual, religion was a big part of my life growing up. But as an adult, I decided on, and adjusted and committed to what was true and real for me. As I learn and grow, I compassionately recommit or adjust my beliefs; otherwise, I feel a spiritual imbalance within myself. Like everything else in life, religious beliefs can grow and blossom.

I believe the behavioral patterns and programs that are rooted in the higher self create an atmosphere that enables us to laugh and be happy and enthusiastic in life, which in turn brings positivity into our life.

Quieting the mind to listen to the heart is not always an easy task. I have lived most of my life thinking and analyzing everything; for me, that is a normal way of life. I have worked a large part of my career analyzing financial records to find discrepancies. Because I am an analytical person, quieting the mind and not evaluating can be difficult. This seems new to me. Yet the reason for quieting the mind is not to ignore or reject any thoughts but to create a pause, so I can connect with my heart.

Using my intuition has helped me to listen and connect to my heart and tap into my spark. Everyone has intuition. It is where you sense and feel without using the rational process, your mind. Some people may feel more intuitive than others, but everyone has the ability to be intuitive if they choose, although at times intuition may feel blocked because of fear, worries, sadness, or low self-esteem.

For example, there was a person at work who could easily make me feel irate. Sometimes I wished that the person would exit my life and never return. I noticed that when we were in conflict, I felt miserable for days. As I began to develop my intuition, I was able to differentiate between my own struggling fears and what my heart was telling me. My intuition was telling me to relax, and everything was going to be okay.

Daily, I use my intuition to figure out what I am feeling and needing without judging myself as right or wrong. It is important to be honest and open with ourselves, whether we are coming from a place of love or fear. Then I believe our intuition will help us connect to our spark, heart, or higher self. Using intuition has led me to where I am today, how I want to move forward, and what I want to create in my life.

I have learned that I can go from operating from my higher self (listening to my heart) to being disconnected from my heart in a matter of minutes. Here are some examples of when I experience a shift of consciousness and go on autopilot behavioral patterns. When my children are fighting continuously throughout the day, I may start out calm and peaceful but later lose my composure and get angry. I especially experience a disconnect and lose energy when my children call each other names or hurt each other. I have the same reaction with people who "press my hot buttons," as for example, when I see people behaving unjustly toward others—taking advantage, devaluing, or oppressing me or another person.

These situations trigger my existing programs *I am not lovable* or *I am not valuable* and I take these situations personally. I notice over and over again how difficult it is for me to avoid my automatic behavioral patterns (the silent whispers of my mind) due to my existing programs. However, the more aware I become of my programs and behavioral patterns, the better I am able to understand them.

Application of Nonviolent Communication Concepts

I find it much easier to fully apply NVC concepts when I am connected to my higher self and listening to my heart. I am better able to observe, to express my feelings and needs, and to make requests. Also, the NVC concepts help me to identify the patterns and programs that don't serve me well and lead me to evaluate. With this new awareness came a deep desire to figure out how to break free from my programs and patterns, which were leading me to communicate violently with myself and others. Applying the NVC concepts allows me to break free from a life of self-sabotage and self-destruction.

In the next chapter I will talk about techniques that have helped me break free and begin to heal. These techniques can bring tremendous encouragement and positive feelings to life!

BREAKING FREE FROM A LIFE OF EVALUATIONS

The next step after awareness of my patterns and programs was to learn how to break free and begin to heal. At first, I thought all I needed to do was to let go of past pain. That was partially true. I used books like *Free to Love, Free to Heal* by David Simon to help me in releasing and healing my existing patterns and programs. Also, Louise Hay's book *You Can Heal Your Life* was very helpful to me in valuing my individuality and honoring myself. These books gave me constructive ways to clean up the clutter in my mind and begin to hear and live from the heart.

However, after a while I noticed new issues surfacing. As soon as I dealt with one issue, another would surface. Or an old issue would resurface as the root cause of what I was experiencing. It seemed like a never-ending battle. I moved through cycles of depression, awareness, letting go, and healing. Finally, I realized that breaking free and healing was a life-long process— a path to peace, love, joy, and balance in my life. This is not to say that I was not already experiencing peace, love, joy, and balance in life. My family and friends view me as a very positive person. But deep inside, I felt something was missing. It caused my body to ache, so that I would bring attention to it. The more aware I became of my programs and patterns, the more I realized that depression had been silently following me throughout my life.

My understanding of my programs and patterns does not always stop me from continuing to live in them, mainly because I am still evaluating, judging, and blaming myself and others. However, just being able to recognize how my evaluations keep popping up in my life is a milestone. I am able to link my silent depression to evaluating, judging, and blaming myself and others. This recognition produces a desire in me to stay aware—to focus on observing what is going in my life. And so I can begin to look for ways to break free from a life of evaluation.

CHAPTER 5: DETOXIFYING THE MIND

Close your eyes and try to imagine the entire sky. The sky is vast, but see the mind as even bigger than the sky. It's a pretty impressive organ, the brain! It is bombarded with stimuli every moment of the day, including thoughts (internal messages, programs) that for the most part are negative. These negative internal thoughts can cause depression and disease. The brain is also bombarded with external messages, such as from television, radio, and the web. These external messages can also affect you significantly, especially if they are negative, because they are intended to influence and persuade you. Therefore, detoxifying your mind of internal and external messages can help you tap into your higher true self and break free from a life of evaluations.

Here are four ways I detoxify my mind:

<u>First Approach</u>

The first way is to turn off the television. That's right, turn it off! The images and messages we get from TV commercials, entertainment shows, and news require no feedback. It is a one-way interaction from the TV to us. The television tells us what we should purchase, what we should eat, and what type of car we should drive. Worst of all, it tries to define beauty for us.

Keep television in mind as you read this quote from the Tao Te Ching:

"When people see some things as beautiful, other things become ugly.

 When people see some things as good, other things become bad. . . .

 If you over-esteem great men, people become powerless.

 If you overvalue possessions, people begin to steal."

I am greatly influenced by television. When I watch an award show, many times I feel insecure afterwards. I start to compare my life with the lives of Hollywood celebrities. I look in the mirror and feel different—feel that something is missing. I am not attractive enough, not wealthy enough, not educated enough, and/or missing out on the glamour life. I am continually devaluing myself, sometimes just for the evening, but sometimes for days until I decide I have had enough grief and snap out of it. When I see sex or receive sexual messages on TV, I want to have sex. It makes me wonder how those images and messages are received by children or by adults who don't have partners. How does that make them feel? I wonder what their self-evaluations are and how that affects their happiness.

Every day the news report on people suffering, the economic crisis, war, murder, stealing. Such images cause stress in my life. Yet these and other graphic images have become a normal part of our external messages. Whenever I watch the news, I feel afraid of something, whether it is fear for my safety, fear of poverty, fear of no control, or fear of the future. Then I am afraid to go out at night or even to be alone. Television messages and images not only create fear but become part of my internal thoughts, which affect how I think and behave, which then define me.

What kind of entertainment is television if it causes me to evaluate myself, compare my life to others, and then get depressed? Also, the electromagnetic waves from the television are enervating. That's why I feel sapped of energy after watching a two-hour movie. Watching TV directly affects my levels of happiness, health, and hope. As a result, I seldom watch movies or TV, but when I do, I focus right away on eliminating the fear, sadness, and pain from my body.

I used to think that TV relaxed me, but now I prefer to spend my time doing something that will inspire me. Try turning off your TV for two weeks and see how you feel. When I stopped watching TV, one thing I did not miss was the constant external influence. I became happier and more satisfied with myself in my own world. I was able be present and gently listen to my own internal messages.

My children watch more TV than I do. Often they tell me, "It's a good thing you didn't watch that program with us. You wouldn't have liked it. It was too violent." As I have limited watching television and listening to radio talk shows, I have substituted other entertainment that empowers me. I enjoy taking walks, exercising, dancing, singing, listening to music, visiting family and friends, calling loved ones, reading books, meditating, and resting by going to sleep early.

Second Approach

Another way I detoxify my mind is a visualization exercise I do to release negativity when I am stuck in a conflict with another person. Doing a visualization exercise helps me cool down, reorganize my thoughts, and see what's important to me. Whether I get into an argument at work, home, or another place, the anger and pain often add up to a tremendous amount of stress.

Visualization helps me pause and empathize with my feelings and needs. Then I am better able to recognize my thoughts and connect with my intention. With the visualization, I am able to release my excess emotions, helping me to think straight and resolve my feelings before moving forward.

Here is an example of how I used a visualization exercise to reorganize and release excess emotions. One time I was at a department meeting, and my boss took credit for my hard work without acknowledging my effort. I felt sad, embarrassed, and furious. I was debating with myself whether to say something during the meeting, but I stayed quiet because I was angry. I was afraid my anger would explode and cost me my job. As a result, I was filled with resentment and plans for revenge. At the same time, I blamed myself for not speaking up. This situation stayed in my mind the entire day. The message kept repeating internally over and over; I was stuck in it. I knew I needed to calm down and organize my thoughts before I talked to my boss, not only for the sake of my job but also for the sake of my health.

I went to a quiet place—closed my eyes and became aware of my breath. I felt heaviness in my chest and pain in my neck but attempted to connect to the stillness within me. I pictured my boss . . . and I stated everything that was on my mind. I let out all of my emotions.

My tirade went something like this: "You jerk! You idiot! You have no right taking credit for my work. How could you treat me like this? Don't you have any conscience? I deserve proper acknowledgment and respect. How dare you! I am furious! You are an absolute Idiot! I hate working for you. You suck and so does your management style. I demand an apology with proper recognition."

Then I said to myself, *"For the sake of my health, I want to get rid of all negative emotions and negative energy from every part of my head and body, from this situation and you. I forgive you and forgive myself. I am now replacing it with positive energy, unconditional love, and light for myself. I hold no anger or resentment toward you."* I had to repeat this exercise until I got all my emotions out and felt understood. Then I opened my eyes.

This visualization exercise was not only a great way for me to release tension, to connect with my intention, and to reorganize my thoughts, but also an opportunity for me to pause and observe my own evaluations. I felt safe to express what I was truly thinking and feeling because I was alone. I felt no pressure, no judgment, no blame from the outside. After doing the exercise, I was already to apply the NVC skills I have learned. I thought back to the meeting and my boss. I replayed and listened to what was said. I translated what I heard and felt, what I need, and how I could request it. I wrote down the conversation I planned to have with my boss, and then I was ready to approach him.

Every time I use this visualization exercise I become more aware of the evaluations, programs, and patterns playing out in my life. Also, the visualization exercise helps me pause and effectively apply the NVC method.

This may sound strange but it's true: I have also noticed in doing the visualization exercise that the other person somehow receives a positive vibe from my internal conversation. It may be because I am able to observe the situation, I feel empowered, and as a result, my empowerment empowers others to feel safe and understood.

There are, of course, some recurring situations where the anger and pain are too overwhelming, and detoxifying the mind gets more complicated. In these situations, a grudge may seem more like the answer. Holding a grudge makes me feel like I am protecting my own dignity. When this happens, my main concern is to first realize how important it is for me to let go of the anger and pain. Usually, I am in serious need of empathy. When I am not able to let go, I become bitter, resentful, and always sick. And that is when a red flag goes up for me: My bitter and sad feelings are a sign that tells me I am harming myself. I am harboring ill thoughts that are poisonous to me and others. To me, harboring negativity in my mind for a long period of time is an act of self-punishment and self-hatred. This is a motivation for me to let go of the issue and look for nonviolent approaches to moving forward. I ask myself, Does it matter who's right or wrong if I end up sick and on medication? I find having the intention to live a healthy and happy life gives me the courage to let go of angry thoughts and then do the visualization exercise.

Third Approach

The third way I detoxify my mind is to do a sweeping exercise. Before I go to bed, I mentally sweep through my mind—through my thoughts and emotions—and I forgive myself and others. Forgiveness is one the biggest gifts I can give myself when I sweep the clutter out of my mind. When I forgive, I feel a release of tension and healing in my mind, body, and soul. Life is short; even if I live to be 100 years old, it will have gone by too fast. Forgiving helps me to eliminate the burden of resentment and revenge and leaves me with peace of mind.

Sometimes when I feel unable to forgive, I become constipated. A friend who is a massage therapist always reminds me "to remove the issues from my tissues," which means not to hold pain and anger in my body and mind. She tells me that if I feel unable to forgive, then to pray and ask for the pain to be taken away from my heart, so that I am able to forgive and move on. When I forgive and let go of the "issues in my tissues," I have a regular bowel movement. Honestly! I am so at ease that at the same I am getting rid of the waste in my mind, I am also getting rid of the waste in my body.

I firmly believe that most diseases are the result of underlying physical, emotional, mental, and spiritual despair. I remember a time in my life where I had severe back pain, which was my physical symptom. At that time I was also emotionally distressed—not receiving the love and emotional support that I wanted from my partner. I discovered that my emotional issues were the cause of my back pain. Since the backbone physically supports the entire body from head to toe, it was negatively affected, because I was feeling unsupported. An interesting connection for me!

I want to share a remarkable quote from Bill Clinton, who wondered if Nelson Mandela had truly forgiven his captors. President Clinton said, "Many years later, I had a chance to ask him. I said, 'Come on, you were a great man, you invited your jailers to your inauguration, you put your pressures on the government. But tell me the truth. Weren't you really angry all over again?'

"And Mandela said, 'Yes, I was angry. And I was a little afraid. After all, I've not been free in so long. But,' he said, 'when I felt anger well up inside of me, I realized that if I hated them after I got outside that gate, then they would still have me.' And he smiled and said, 'I wanted to be free, so I let it go.'

"It was an astonishing moment in my life. It changed me."

In my experience, forgiving myself and others has also changed my life for the better. As a result, I am able to release a whole lot of tension and focus on the what? —on what I have today. In forgiving, I remember that people are hurting and not to take their actions personally, so I look deeper into their hearts. At the same time, I realize I am hurting too, and I don't want to hurt any more! I want to free myself from pain and live in the present connected to my higher self. The NVC skills help me forgive when I apply them. Using them confirms that all people have similar feelings and needs. So when I am in conflict with someone, identifying the feelings and needs helps me to see the human side of the other person.

Fourth Approach

The fourth and most challenging way I detoxify my mind is useful when I get so irritated or upset at someone that I ask myself this question: "What do I hate so much about myself that I see in this person?"

This can be a difficult question to ask and answer. It requires me to be honest, brave, and vulnerable. I notice many times the things that I hate the most about others are the things I (consciously or unconsciously) hate most about myself in the present or have hated in the past. For example, I hate it when people are inconsiderate to me because I hate it when I am inconsiderate to myself. I hate it when people are parsimonious, because I used to be frugal and did not believe I had abundance. Now that I feel abundance in my life, I hate it when I see frugality in others.

I believe other people mirror our thoughts and feelings and how we treat ourselves. Maybe that's why we are unable to see ourselves and need a mirror to see our reflection. I notice that by reflecting on the things I hate and looking into my past insecurities, I can take ownership of my thoughts. As a result, this helps me to look into the hearts of others. It's a strange paradigm. I notice when I am feeling sad, my children are sad. When I have a positive outlook on life, often they have a positive attitude too. Worst of all, when I am angry everyone around me seems to be angry.

Recently, I was in a conflict with my oldest son. He was giving me ultimatums. He said, "If you don't take me to the store to buy a sweatshirt, I won't do my homework or study for my test." I was very upset, confused, and scared. I did not find much online to help me understand why teenagers give their parents ultimatums. So I decided to call a friend and tell him about what was going on. He asked me, "Is your son mirroring your behavior?" I wasn't expecting my friend to be so direct about it. He asked me if I communicated by giving ultimatums. The answer was yes. I was communicating and resolving my frustrations by giving my son ultimatums. I would say things like,

"If you don't do your homework, you can't watch TV or play any games." "If you do not behave, you will not be able to see your friends. Be good and you can see them."

It's not always fun finding out how people are mirroring me, especially in this case with my son. But after the initial shock was over, I was relieved by and joyful at my new awareness. I sat down with my son and spoke to him about ultimatums. I apologized for communicating with him that way and requested we both consider each others feelings. Fortunately, as I changed my communication pattern, my son changed his too.

There are times, of course, when I just can't comprehend how the other person could possibly be mirroring my behavior. Many times this happens with someone I perceive to be very different from me. For example, there was a person in my life whose behavioral pattern when angry was to stay angry for months, never admitting a mistake and never forgiving. This person was also verbally abusive. I completely refused to see how this person could ever have been mirroring me. In such a case, I first try to accept the person the way he or she is. If I can, that's great. If I can't, then I move to the second option—I get help from outside myself. It could be talking with a friend, going to counseling, getting some coaching or training, or whatever I need to resolve my feelings. I also meditate and pray for direction on how to deal with the person. In the end, I know I can't change anyone but myself. Many times when I am frustrated, I say to myself "I love, accept, and approve of myself completely." I get inner strength from that affirmation that helps me to approve of and accept others the way they are.

These are the four ways I detoxify my mind. They help me to separate myself from negativity and negative energy, which become barriers to the truth of who I am and what I am capable of achieving. Detoxifying the mind helps me break free from a life of evaluation (free from old programs and patterns). The NVC method also helps me to get rid of the nonsense clutter in my mind, connect to my higher self, and come from a place of love, confidence, and safety (from the silent whispers of my heart).

CHAPTER 6: HEALING USING THE SCRIPT

As I became more aware of my programs and patterns, I noticed that it is important for me to take 100% responsibility and accountability for my own actions and behaviors, for my feelings, thoughts, beliefs, and attitudes. I understand that my feelings are neither good nor bad. They are what they are, and they are a result of a deeper need or desire.

Karol K. Truman talks about choosing whether we want to be a *victim* or a *master* of our destiny in her book *Feelings Buried Alive Never Die*. She advises to stop looking for answers outside ourselves and instead to look within to gain control of what causes our challenges, problems, and negative programs and patterns. To explain the Epictetus quote, "No man is free who is not master of himself," Truman says that "taking accountability allows a great shift of major proportions, one that allows you to become the master of your Self and your universe. All that is necessary is to be willing to be accountable for:

1. Your own feelings
2. Your own thoughts
3. Your own words
4. Your own actions

By choosing to let go of blame and judgment, you start on your road to becoming a more responsible and accountable person." She further explains that becoming responsible and accountable is necessary to overcome the "victim" role in life. It puts control back into our life. So the attitude of a master is that there is nothing out there, not a person or a thing, that is the cause of my problems. All the causes of my problems in life are from within myself.

In my experience it seems easier playing the role of victim than playing the role of master in life. When playing the victim, I had all kinds of supporters and an audience that wanted to console me and try to fix my problems. When playing the role of master, on the other hand, I found fewer supporters and no audience, because I took full responsibility for what I was thinking and feeling. It was quite different for me to blame no one but rather to look within for answers. In the long run, playing the master role has generated peace in my life. Truman describes seven behaviors for being a master:

1. LETTING GO of the blame and judgment
2. LETTING GO of force and control
3. FORGIVING completely
4. LOVING unconditionally
5. ACCEPTING challenges with gratitude
6. ACCEPTING the perfection in everyone and everything
7. GIVING thanks in all things

Truman also talks about scripting as a tool, as a one-sided reasoning with your Higher Self. The purpose of the script is to replace the negative feelings with positive feelings. She refers to each person as being born with a perfect blueprint and using the script to go back to a positive life force. It brought tears to my eyes when I read in Truman's book that she has found in her coaching practice "that practically everyone (on a subconscious level) does NOT love themselves. They do not accept themselves nor trust themselves. Most of these same people don't even like themselves. Interestingly enough, they all THINK they like, love, accept, and trust themselves."

I could see this to be true about myself. I was living a life of self-sabotage, and I wanted to start loving and accepting myself. I was ready to return to my perfect blueprint. I wanted to be present in living in my true self.

I'd like to share the scripts from Truman's book that I use to process any uncomfortable feelings. It is very helpful to have the script copied down, so it can be used wherever and whenever. It has become part of my life, giving me the boost I need to remember how important and special I am, and making me aware of living from my true, Higher Self.

Truman suggests going to a quiet and comfortable place to do the script. Here is a blank script. Later I will insert the negative and positive feelings in the script. You address your Higher Self, your Spirit or Super-Conscious—whatever you like to call it. I like to call to my Higher Self. Feel free to replace or adjust the script to your religious or educational beliefs.

"Higher self, please locate the origin of my feeling(s)/thought(s) of
(a)_____.
Take each and every level, layer, area, and aspect of my Being to this origin. Analyze and resolve it perfectly with God's truth.
Come through all generations of time and eternity, healing every incident and its appendages based on the origin. Do it according to God's will until I'm at the present—filled with light and truth, God's peace and love, forgiveness of myself for my incorrect perceptions, forgiveness of every person, place, circumstance, and event which contributed to this feeling(s)/
thought(s).
With total forgiveness and unconditional love, I allow every physical, mental, emotional, spiritual, and ethereal problem, and inappropriate behavior based on the negative origin recorded in my DNA, to transform.
(b) I Choose BE-ing

_____.

(c) I Feel
_____
___.
(d) I AM
_____
_____.
It is done. It is healed. It is accomplished now!

Thank you, Higher Self, for coming to my aid and helping me attain the full measure of my creation. Thank you, thank you, thank you! I love you and praise my Creator from whom all blessings flow."

State the negative feeling in the first blank (a) and positive feelings in the next three blanks (b, c, d) to replace the first negative feeling. Here is an example from Truman's book for the negative feelings that keep me from liking and loving myself:

"*Higher Self, please locate the origin of my feeling(s)/thought(s) that keep me from liking and loving myself.*
Take each and every level, layer, area, and aspect of my Being to this origin. Analyze and resolve it perfectly with God's truth.
Come through all generations of time and eternity, healing every incident and its appendages based on the origin. Do it according to God's will until I'm at the present—filled with

*light and truth, God's peace and love,
forgiveness of myself for my incorrect
perceptions, forgiveness of every person, place,
circumstance, and event which contributed to
this feeling (s)/thoughts(s).
With total forgiveness and unconditional love, I
allow every physical, mental, emotional,
spiritual, and ethereal problem, and
inappropriate behavior based on the negative
origin recorded in my DNA, to transform.
I choose liking myself. I feel likable. I AM liking
myself. I choose loving myself. I feel love for
myself. I AM loving myself. I give myself
permission to like and love myself. I feel worthy
of this love.
It is done. It is healed. It is accomplished now!
Thank you, higher self, for coming to my aid
and helping me attain the full measure of my
creation. Thank you, thank you, thank you! I
love you and praise my Creator from whom all
blessings flow."*

Now, using the original blank script, I repeat it for the negative feelings that keep me from accepting myself and trusting myself: "Higher self, please locate the origin of the feelings that keep me from accepting myself and trusting myself." I continue through the Script until I come to the next blank line, replacing the negative words with words to this effect: "I choose to accept myself unconditionally. I feel acceptance of myself. I AM accepting myself. I choose trusting myself implicitly! I feel total faith and trust in myself. I AM trusting myself. I am my best supporter." Then I finish the rest of script."

Another negative feeling I thought it was important to use the script for was to reprogram failure: "Higher self, please locate the origin of the feelings that cause me to continually fail."

I go through the rest of the script and insert the following at lines b, c, and d: I choose succeeding. I feel successful. I AM succeeding. I choose reprogramming myself for success. I am succeeding in all my endeavors. I AM successful!" Then I finish the script."

Truman states,

This does not necessarily mean that all of a sudden you are going to go   out and succeed in everything you do. It is still necessary to observe and adhere to correct principles in your feelings and thoughts in order to succeed. However, reprogramming yourself to succeed opens up the channels to help eliminate the saboteurs that have been keeping you from meeting your desired goals."

I find the script to be a useful tool for healing and reprogramming and to start to create new, positive patterns. Truman shares in detail many examples of how to utilize the script. I want to share two more:

"... *locate the origin of feelings that cause my incorrect use of judgment or my incorrect use of wisdom.*" *A possible replacement would be, I choose opening my mind and heart to truth. I feel able to open my mind and heart to trust. I am opening my mind and heart to truth. I choose accepting trust. I feel like accepting the truth. I am accepting truth. I choose making correct decisions. I feel able to make correct decisions. I am making correct decisions. I accept truth and extend trust with all my heart."* Then finish the script.

"... *locate the origin of my feelings that cause me to identify with my possessions and have little sense of self.*" *Replace with something like,* "*I choose finding my own identity. I feel like finding my own identity. I am finding my own identity. I feel a great sense of self. I feel love and respect for myself. I am loving and honoring myself just the way I am."* Then finish the script.

Next, I took my programs of *I am not lovable, I am not worthy, I am not fun*, and *I have no choice* and scripted with them. I find the script to be a great tool that gives me back my own original power to reprogram my programs and create new, positive patterns. The script enables me to access my higher self. I can talk to my higher self and take control of my thinking, feeling, and action. I absolutely love using the script.

Chapter 7: Healing Using Affirmations

Affirmations allow me to stay positive and avoid evaluations and judging. Affirmations are something I say to myself to confirm the truth. They are similar to using the script, though in script I am replacing my negative feelings with positive feelings, and in using affirmations I am making a positive statement to boost my self-esteem.

I became interested in this technique when I learned that all of the thoughts I think in a day become my affirmations. It was scary to think that all of my self-talk, my inner-dialogue, is a flow of affirmations that I confirm and believe in each day. So, if my self-talk is self-critical, my affirmations are self-critical. I want to come from a state of unconditional love for myself.

I noticed that when I said certain affirmations, I felt better about myself. It was almost like a special gift I was giving myself, stating affirmations with sincerity and with intention. As a result, I find that affirmations bring encouragement for and positive feelings about my self-worth.

Alone with the script, I use affirmations such as *I am lovable, I am worthy, I am fun,* and *I choose powerfully in my life.* My positive affirmations list grows and changes as I become more in tune with my feelings and needs. I create new ones to support myself in attaining goals and enhance areas such as health, love, abundance, joy, and peace.

To enhance positive thinking, I choose one positive affirmation and repeat it several times a day. I have added positive affirmations to my prayers and meditation, which help me make a deeper connection. I notice that when I repeat affirmations this way, I discover more programs, patterns, and self-sabotaging behavior, in which case I use the script as well.

The following affirmations from www.vitalaffirmations.com provided a great start when I began practicing this technique:

Affirmations for Health
- Every cell in my body vibrates with energy and health.
- Loving myself heals my life. I nourish my mind, body, and soul.
- My body heals quickly and easily.

Affirmations for Abundance
- I prosper wherever I turn and I know that I deserve prosperity of all kinds.
- The more grateful I am, the more reasons I find to be grateful.

- I pay my bills with love as I know abundance flows freely through me.

Affirmations for Love
- I know that I deserve Love and accept it now.
- I give out Love and it is returned to me multiplied.
- I rejoice in the Love I encounter every day.

Affirmations for Romance
- I have a wonderful partner and we are both happy and at peace.
- I release any desperation and allow love to find me.
- I attract only healthy relationships.

Affirmations for Weight Loss
- I am the perfect weight for me.
- I choose to make positive healthy choices for myself.
- I choose to exercise regularly.

Affirmations for Self-Esteem
- When I believe in myself, so do others.
- I express my needs and feelings.
- I am my own unique self—special, creative, and wonderful.

Affirmations for Peace and Harmony

- All my relationships are loving and harmonious.
- I am at peace.
- I trust in the process of life.

Affirmations for Joy and Happiness
- Life is a joy filled with delightful surprises.
- My life is a joy filled with love, fun, and friendship. All I need do is stop all criticism, forgive, relax, and be open.
- I choose love, joy, and freedom, to open my heart and allow wonderful things to flow into my life.

My favorite affirmations from Louise Hay's book *You Can Heal Your Life* are the following:

I approve of myself! I love you. I really love you. I love myself therefore . . . I am worthy. I am valuable, I am lovable. I am willing to let go. I release. I let go. I release all tension. I release all fear. I release all anger, I release all guilt. I release all sadness. I let go and I am at peace. I am at peace with myself. I am peace with the process of life. I am safe. I am lovable. I have everything I want in life. I am worthy. I am fun. I choose powerfully. My life is fair and great. Everything is working in Divine Right order. All is well. I am willing to release the need for uncomfortable relationship. I approve of myself. I am willing to forgive. I love myself, therefore I forgive my past. I am willing to release the patterns in me that created these conditions. I am in the process of positive change. I have a happy, slender body. I am healthy, whole, and complete. I experience love wherever I go. I have the prefect living space. I appreciate all that I do. I trust the process of life to bring me the highest good and greatest joy. I deserve the best and I accept the best now. I am deeply fulfilled with by all I do. Every experience is a success. I listen with love to my body's messages.

She also talks about scripting with the following method:
I choose to be _____. I feel _____ and I am _____.
Fill in the blanks: worthy, in love, loved freely, in control.

Saying positive affirmations helps me nurture positive thoughts and creates a positive atmosphere for my thoughts to dwell in. I have discovered when saying affirmations to also speak to myself, using "you" as well as "I," which makes a deeper connection for me. When I say "you," I feel my higher-self talking to me and reassuring me. For example, I say the following affirmations to myself: "I love you. You are worthy." "I love you. You are important." "I love you. You are good enough." The affirmation "You are" seems to be the key for me. I feel a sense of reassurance coming from the inside as well from the outside of me. That's why when I am down and depressed, the affirmation "I am worthy" sometimes doesn't convince me but "You are worthy" does. As I continue to say positive affirmations, they help me in breaking free from some of my self-critical patterns and programs and a life of constant evaluations.

Chapter 8: Healing Using Energy Cards

I was fortunate to meet Denise Malayeri who talked about the benefits of using energy cards. Denise talked about taking 5-by-7 index cards to write down affirmations. Energy cards have been useful to me in generating positive energy for a specific goal. Here are the instructions Denise gave to create energy cards for finding a job.

1. Let your mind be at peace, breathe deeply:
   - Let go of all expectations placed on you by other people
   - Let go of your own limiting thinking
   - Let go of the past (except the wisdom of the past)

2. List the information requested on 5-by-7 cards and place in multiple sites:
   - bedside
   - car
   - daytime planner/calendar/purse
   - bathroom

3. Visualize the perfect work and workplace for you (think outside of the box—not what is possible or likely but what you really want). Answer the following questions on your 5-by-7 cards (be as specific as possible):
   - What kind of work do you see yourself doing?

- What kind of environment would you like to work in—an office with windows, outdoors in nature?
- What kind of leader do you want?
- What kind of co-workers would you like to work with?
- What's the mix of male and female energy?
- What is the income level?
- What kind of attire do you see yourself wearing?
- What components are important in your work?
- What distance would you like to travel to work?
- What are you passionate about?

Copy your list and write a closing positive affirmation and place in multiple sites.

4. This process needs to incubate until your ideas are hatched. Until you have had a few weeks to reflect on your visualization, you need to keep the process a secret. Once you've allowed yourself time to let the ideas become clearer, then have someone you trust read what you've written slowly and out loud, until you feel like you've completely covered all that's important to you. Edit your card as new aspects come to light. When complete, you may want to laminate the card.

5. Somewhere on your cards, prepare two short affirmations—one as an opening and one as a closing.
   - Opening: Acknowledges that this work is a perfect match for you. Example: "I now declare this perfect, holy work is a match with my talents and allows me to be a blessing to the world for the highest good."
   - Closing: Accepts that this work is already presenting itself to you and you recognize it now. Example: "I am grateful for all of the opportunities already presenting themselves to me and for the willingness to see the right and perfect job for me NOW. Create the opening for me so I can step into it."

6. Preferably write the cards and affirmations in your own handwriting. That seems to really imprint it in your mind and, therefore, in the Universe.

7. Read through and speak all that is on your cards at least three times per day. Remember that the perfect work for you is already out there or in the process of materializing, and you just have to be open to receiving it. At the time I was unemployed, so I decided to create my own energy card. Here is what it said:

Thank you for this opportunity. I now declare this perfect, holy work is a match with my talents and allows me to be a blessing to the world, with Love for the highest good!

Work:	Co-workers:
–Publish minded	–Open
–Spiritual	–Caring
–Motivational integrity/honest	–High
–Healing myself and others	–Able to laugh
–Independent Flexible	–
–Manageable amount of work	–Fun
	Dress:
Casual/comfortable	
Environment:	Salary:
–Light $100,000 or greater	–

-Friendly
Benefits (insurance & retirement -Open plan)

-Windows

-Casual / comfortable

-Able to see trees

Leader:
    Distance:

-Empowering of staff   -Work from home

-High ideals

-Easygoing

-High integrity/honest

-Spiritual

I am grateful for all of the opportunities already presenting themselves to me and for the willingness to see the right and perfect job for me NOW! Create the opening for me now so I can step into it.

I read my energy cards often. Several days later, I had a deep desire to start writing this book. I had one opening after another about what to write.

Then I came to what is called a "writer's block." I didn't know what else to write about. I didn't have any leads on publishing. I stopped reading the energy cards, and I became uninterested in finishing my book. I didn't know what to else to do.

Three months later I went to visit my dear cousin in California. I met a good friend there. He introduced me to the nonviolent communication books. I was pretty impressed with the fellow, so I ordered the books and started reading. After I completed reading a series of NVC books, I had a desire to reorganize my own book. I also rediscovered the desire to read my energy cards. I began to edit this book and to include NVC concepts in it. Energy cards are great way to narrow down what you desire and bring about new openings in life.

Chapter 9: Healing by Connecting to the Earth

Connecting to the earth is becoming aware of and reflecting and appreciating my surroundings (the living organisms), which enable me to live more in the present and heal. Connecting to nature helps me to see a broader view and to live in admiration of and gratitude for animals, plants, and myself. Connecting to the earth helps me to realize how my evaluations are limiting barriers that prevent me from connecting to my higher self and others (people, nature, and all living things). I have always thought of myself as a person who cares for animals and the environment. Then, several years ago, I came across Hakim Archuletta's writings on natural health and healing. I learned completely new concepts about becoming earth-connected. Archuletta talks about being fully present in our surroundings and then appreciating them as a key piece of good health. He calls it BEING ALIVE!

Archuletta explains that the Earth is made up of two components: land (which is dirt or dust) and water, which is the oceans, lakes, or rivers. We human beings are also made from the same two components: dirt or dust and water. In essence, we are the Earth. That is why when people die they are buried—returned to the Earth. So humans already have a form of connection with the Earth. When the earth is clean and healthy, it allows us to live a cleaner, healthier, and fulfilled life. On the other hand, as the Earth becomes polluted, human lives are directly affected. Archuletta further shares "that everything you find inside this body, you will find outside of that body in some form (in perfect reflection)—not one hair more or one hair less from the animals, trees, and plants."

Archuletta talks about looking at animals and reflecting on them to learn similarities. Each animal has a function and a characteristic that can reveal various traits within our human nature. He gave as an example some people who appear as people on the outside but who are cobras, striking at whoever comes close. Others are like scorpions that sting. Some resemble peacocks, always dressed excessively, wanting attention and arrogant about their beauty. Some are like the clever fox or the meek sheep. How about the mouse that steals when no one is looking? I don't think the purpose of these reflections is to label yourself or other people as animals. It was hard at first for me to resist pairing up people with animals, especially people I viewed as being in deep pain or having emotional trauma. But because I realized that doing so allowed me to play victim and kept me focused and stuck on my own pain, I decided instead to be in awe of this natural connection that exists between humans and animals and to observe it simply for what it is.

In particular, Archuletta pointed to the connection we have with horses. He has worked with patients suffering from severe clinical depression and their contact with horses bought them great healing. So not only do animals share similar characteristics with us, but they also can help us in the healing process. I have seen many times where house pets such as cats, dogs, and birds were able to sense their owners' emotions. When their owners are depressed, the pets sit quietly nearby or have contact with them to cheer them up. I once had a student whose parents were divorced. He told me that when he was very depressed, his parakeet used to come and sit on his shoulder. I believe the parakeet was sensing my student's emotions and helping him heal.

Recently, I experienced a similar healing and connection with animals and plants at the zoo. For several years in a row I have volunteered to go with my children on zoo field trips. Previously, I had only experienced extremely energetic children at the beginning and extremely exhausted children at the end of the trips. Recently, though, when I accompanied my daughter's class to the zoo, I experienced a healing of my body, accompanied by a sense of calm. I was tired, but I sensed a great inner peace. When I first walked into the zoo, I had been feeling a sense of heaviness with all my worries. I was feeling sad about certain things that were going on in my life. After being in the zoo for a while, walking through nature, and watching and coming into contact with all different kinds of animals and trees, I started feeling cheerful. By the end of the zoo visit I felt lighter, and much if not all of my tension was alleviated. It was a wonderful experience.

Have you ever wondered why the sky is blue and the grass is green? Imagine if the sky were red and the grass were black. How would it feel driving to work with a red sky? The movies show a red sky when they want to show danger or the world coming to an end. The colors in nature are amazingly calming to my eyes, and when observed and valued they bring about a healing for me.

How about the different shades, colors, textures, and smells of flowers that exist? For example, there are so many different shades of greenery, textures, and scents in the trees. There are so many different colors of fragrant flowers in nature. My life is enhanced when I choose to be aware of and be present to these living organisms around me. The brightness of the sunlight can brighten my day if I let it. Cold fresh water satisfies my thirst when I drink it. The benefits of connecting to Nature are endless.

Further, I can choose to reflect on my own body in this same way. I recognize that being able to stand is miraculous thing. Here is all my body weight, which I can control and maneuver smoothly. My voice is amazing. I can talk, change my tone, sing, laugh, cry, scream. What an amazing ability! How about the breath? What a huge blessing it is that we can breathe in and out automatically.

These reflections have endlessly remarkable abilities to help us live in the present moment and bring great appreciation in our lives. To experience all of this reflection and connection with animals, nature, and self is indeed a key to good health.

Archuletta states that a person can be on the best diet, do the best exercise, and study from the greatest books, but if they don't have thanks and praise for things, they won't and can't be well. I found a great way to becoming more earth-connected is to keep a gratitude journal. For a while I wrote things daily that I was grateful for. As I wrote in my journal, I became more aware of my surroundings. I began to see things I had never noticed. I reflected on and made connections with the positive things in my life. When I don't have time to write in a daily journal, I try to commit to writing a daily gratitude statement. Today my gratitude statement is, "I am grateful for the joy my three children bring to my life." It could be about anything. Yesterday, my gratitude statement was, "I am grateful for clean water."

When I go outside, I try to quiet my mind and take a moment to become more conscious of the Earth and its surroundings, to become Earth-connected. Here are some of the things I do to connect to the Earth: I sit outside and listen to the birds sing. I lie outside and watch the sky. I watch the rabbits and squirrels in my backyard. I touch the trees in my yard. I try my best to connect to the Earth through the animals, trees, and plants all around me. My favorite is to walk barefooted on the grass in my yard and on the concrete around my house.

When I stay indoors, I try to spend some quiet time reflecting on myself, my amazing abilities, or my comforts such as electricity, furniture, heat, and so on. Just becoming aware of the gift of five senses—that I can hear, talk, touch, see, and taste. I am amazing! I want to fall in love with myself and be my own number-one fan. It's like discovering myself all over again, like I did for the first time as a child. Observe, reflect, and connect.

I found that connecting to the Earth helps me become present in my life, allowing me to appreciate and connect with what I have. At the same time, I don't have a desire to evaluate myself and others. Connecting to the Earth helps me to heal and break free from a life of evaluation. Moreover, being earth-connected has helped me to live a more positive, healthy, and happy life.

LIVING A LIFE THROUGH OBSERVATIONS

Chapter 10: Learning to Dream

When I was in elementary school, my teachers used to complain to my parents that I daydreamed in class. I remember being a very vibrant child. I definitely knew how to dream while I was awake! I had enough enthusiasm and perseverance to light up a city block. I remember the adults could sense it and would comment on how they felt around me, how I had a positive affect on them. As a child I was used to living from the heart. That's all I knew. There were no limitations, no boundaries--until, of course, I experienced pain and worrying, and then I started to build my own limitations and boundaries and began living off of FEAR, the silent whispers of my mind.

I became a very serious teenager and then a more serious adult. As a teenager I hardly ever liked children. Later as an adult, when I had my own, I realized how serious I had become. I had a hard time being around children. When my son and daughter were playing and laughing, I used to become easily irritated. I had a hard time laughing and playing with them.

Today, I work to bring back the original me, the one who used to dream while I was awake and break free from my more recent limitations and boundaries. I believe that it is healthy to dream while awake; it creates hope. As I continuously go through the process of healing and returning to my true self, I notice that it is easier to experience a dream wholeheartedly when I start living a life of observations.

Here are three tips on how I have learned to dream while awake:

Step 1

First of all, love, respect, and honor yourself and others. When I do, I am able to dream without limitation. The only limitations I have are the ones I put on myself. A great way I bring awareness to how I am treating myself is the way I am treating others. They are connected. When I have love and respect for myself, then that is what I offer to others. When I have lack of self-love and self-respect, I often lack offering it to others. Because I notice if I am kind to myself, it is much easier for me to be kind to others. If I am hard on or judgmental of myself, it is easier for me to be hard on and judgmental of others.

Why do people fall it love with other people who treat them harshly or disrespectfully? Could it be that often people don't respect themselves, have low self-esteem and low self-worth, and so that's what they attract? The connection is so close and accurate that it seems scary at times. It is very important that we first love and respect ourselves, then look for it outside ourselves. Truly honoring ourselves through love and respect will give us the confidence to dream big without limitations, to become the beautiful spiritual beings that we are!

Step 2

Daily read or listen to something that is inspiring. It could be an inspirational book, a holy book, or an inspirational quote that brings you spiritual satisfaction. It could be spending time with a friend who inspires and helps you see things in a new light. Being inspired can help a person stay positive in life, be healed physically, and dream without limitation.

Remember, it doesn't matter where we are in life. Never be discouraged.

> **I believe that we are always right where we are supposed to be, and by daily readings or inspiration we can improve**

our quality of life, allowing us to dream big.

> I have signed up for daily inspirational quotes from PSI Seminars (Personal Success and Personal Development Seminars), which are called "thought of the day." Today's PSI "thought of the day" was "You're braver than you believe and stronger than you seem and smarter than you think" (Christopher Robin to Pooh).

Yesterday's PSI thought of day was "When you judge another, you do not define them, you define yourself. (Wayne Dyer)

Another PSI quote is "We either make ourselves miserable, or we make ourselves strong. The amount of work is the same." (Carlos Castaneda)

I look forward to reading these quotes daily because they bring gentle reminders to me. Also, I read books to keep me inspired and motivated. I read my holy book, which brings me comfort and satisfaction, along with many other great books that have helped me to believe in myself and learn to dream. *The Rest of Your Life: Finding Repose in the Beloved* by John-Roger and Paul Kaye helps me bypass my mind and reach into my loving heart. The book describes what I call the Higher Self or the spark of the Divine as the Beloved that exist within us. Here is an uplifting message from the book:

Put Aside Your Conditions. One day you will at the knowing that you have been walking with the Beloved. You always have and you always will, because the soul is the Beloved. And the one who is self-aware is the manifestation of the Beloved. This is your birthright. You have a right to reach into yourself and find the God of your heart and a right to let others do the same thing.

The loving heart comes from God, from the Beloved. No one can create love. Love is. When it shows up, we drop everything and go with it, because it never leads us astray or into lust, greed, or vanity. It doesn't abuse or take advantage of others, it leads to God. Love is the bliss consciousness in the heart. It brings health and vitality. It brings the opportunity to have all things.

Bring your attention to your breath and allow yourself to let go. Through your breathing, release any futility. Release any dilemma you may have. Release the pressure of seeking for something outside of yourself. Release any worry or concern.

Allow yourself to be in the presence of the Beloved. Assume you are there, even though you may not feel anything. Allow yourself to receive the unconditional loving of the Beloved into you. This unconditional loving is endless, infinite. This is the Beloved singing its own song.

This unconditional loving can't be found by searching, because it is already here, entirely present. Through your breathing, release any pressure around the heart and the back.

Open, receive, and listen to the Beloved singing inside of you.

Do not be concerned about anyone around you, but lift in your loving heart, and there we will all meet as one. And we will be known by this sacred word and presence, the Beloved. In this Beloved, we see all who are Beloved. Just relax and rest in the presence now.

<u>Step 3</u>

Finally, when dreams do come true, accept that you deserve it and avoid both the ego trap and the false humility. The ego trap is believing that we are superior to others and thinking less of others. The false humility is denying the importance of ourselves and minimizing what we do. The ego trap and false humility are both extremes—polar opposites that come from the fear generated by the mind. Acceptance comes from love generated by the heart. Obviously, coming from a place of love is healthier for our entire being.

The following Marianne Williamson quote is a great reminder of false humility and the ego trap, because it proves in a unique way that we all are very special, yet not better than any other. And when one person unlocks how very special they are, it then gives others the courage to do the same.

Our deepest fear is not that we are inadequate. Our deepest fear is that we are powerful beyond measure.

It is our light, not our darkness, that most frightens us. We ask ourselves, "Who am I to be brilliant, gorgeous, talented, fabulous?" Actually, who are you not to be? You are a child of God. Your playing small does not serve the world.

There is nothing enlightened about shrinking so that other people won't feel insecure around you.

We are all meant to shine, as children do. We were born to make manifest the glory of God that is within us. It's not just in some of us; it's in everyone.

And as we let our own light shine, we unconsciously give other people permission to do the same.

As we are liberated from our own fear, our presence automatically liberates others.

I had to read this quote a couple of times to completely comprehend it. It has a powerful message. Were we nurtured as children to think that we are powerful beyond measure? I think for the most part people are hurting, and they unintentionally pass on their fears and limitations to others.

Marianne Williamson's kind of empowerment is often not present and if it is present, it is not taken seriously. As children, we may be a product of our environment, but as adults, we are a product of our choices. For that reason, it is important for adults to choose to nurture the self, to love the self. We can become our own number-one fan! Only we can truly empower ourselves, because no one else knows us better than we do. Learning to listen to our heart and to our intuition will help us to dream without limitation! Dreaming enables us to have hope in our lives and to get our needs met.

Chapter 11: Being Positive and Living in the Present

I have learned that I can't change the past, and I don't know the future, so why let it occupy my present moment? Staying positive has helped me to live in the present moment while observing others. Why suffer in misery, evaluating everything and everyone? Because how much of that can we change?

The choice is ours. No one can make us feel anything without our permission. Don't mind what others think or say to you! Because people are deeply hurting, we are deeply hurting in some shape or form. It's what we do with what others say that is important. It is what we think about (how we observe life) and what we say to ourselves that is important. Let's keep our power with us, take responsibility for our own happiness, and avoid giving power away to others. Responsibility means our **response** to our **ability** to being our own master.

Karol Truman talks about living in the present, living in "the now," how feelings buried alive never die." Many of us go through life so anxiously awaiting the next phase that we do not allow ourselves to be happy or satisfied in the "now." She gives this example,

When we're in grade school, we can hardly wait until we're in junior high school. Then we're in junior high and can't wait until we're in high school. In our early teens, we can hardly wait to be 16 so we can drive a car. Then we're waiting to graduate from high school, to leave home, then to get married, etc. We seldom, if ever, are able to be satisfied and content enjoying the here and now.

She points out that it's important to consider this:

How many of us seem to think that in order for life to work for us, that first we have to HAVE something before we can DO something before we can BE something? For example, do we think that we have to HAVE money so we can DO the fun things in life that we want to do, so we can BE happy? In reality it's just the other way around. We are better off BE-ing first, so that we can DO, so that we can HAVE. HAVING is a natural by-product of BE-ing.

I agree with Truman that life works best in that order—by BE-ing, Doing, and then Having. It makes total sense. For too long, I have lived waiting for tomorrow, for my future to change, to be different, to be bright, and to have more satisfaction. I am ready now to be that change, to be my brightness, to feel more satisfaction today. I don't want to wait, because I don't know if things are going to change tomorrow. All I know is I am ready to change, to live in the present, to live in the now.

Truman states,

Just what does BE-ing refer to? BE forgiving. BE non-judgmental. BE accepting. BE loving. BE grateful. BE caring. BE understanding. BE happy. BE willing to admit you don't know everything. BE the best you can BE everyday. BE efficient, DO the best job, HAVE the best pay. Little by little you can BE-come the kind of person that is most desirable for you to BE, then you will automatically DO the best you can DO. Let me say that one more time: When you are BE-ing the kind of person that is most desirable for you to BE, then you will automatically DO the best you can DO—then you will HAVE the peace and whatever else is most desirable in life for you to HAVE. Therefore, instead of HAVING . . . DOING . . . BEING, life works in better harmony when you are BEING . . . DOING . . . HAVING. After all, you are NOT a human HAVE-ing nor a Human DO-ing. You are a human BE-ing.

Another helpful PSI Seminars tip I remember and live by is to HAVE NO REGRETS IN LIFE. The reason for this is that having regrets traps us in the past, where it is easy to constantly beat up ourselves for what was done or what was not done. Therefore, each night before I go to sleep, I tell myself I did the best I could today. This helps me to let go of the negative and stay positive. Also, telling myself that I did the best I could each day really motivates me to do even better the next day. The reality is that my best can change from moment to moment. It is different when I am healthy as opposed to sick. It is different when I am feeling safe and loved as opposed to feeling fearful and threatened. Under any circumstance, by simply affirming that I am doing my best, I feel happy that I am doing the best of my ability and at the same time can avoid self-judgment, self-abuse, and regret.

Recently, I had some difficulty getting my son and daughter to cooperate with each other. They seem to be willing to consider each others needs and feelings. Too often I end up getting angry and expressing angry words, though at the end of the day, I tell myself I did the best I could, according to what I was feeling and needing. I feel a sense of relief from critical, judgmental evaluations. I am able to observe the situation and plan ahead to use the nonviolent communication strategies of expressing my needs and feelings and helping them do the same. For those times that regret is harbored, I turn to forgiving myself and/or seeking forgiveness—whatever I need to do to let go and break free from self-judgment, self-abuse, and regret.

Of course this does not mean that I do not worry about things. Even when I am free of self-judgment, self-abuse, and regret I may be worrying about something, maybe my family, friends, job, future, pets, or finances. For that reason I have a scheduled worry time. I pick a time during the day, sometimes in the morning as I wake up, or at night before I go to sleep. During this time, I worry about everything in my life that I think is not right, whatever is bothering me that day. Once I worry about it, I like to release the worry by blessing it with a positive thought or prayer that all will work out as it supposed to. And if the same worry comes to me again during the next day, I can think to myself I have already spent energy worrying about this and bless it with a prayer again.

In the attempt to take good care of myself physically, mentally, and spiritually, I want to start by being impeccable with my self-talk. I understand the powerful effects of my self-talk and what it can do for me. Therefore, whenever my mind is silent, I like to fill my time by chanting positive affirmations about myself silently. It's like a special gift I give myself throughout the day to make myself conscious of my true self. I enjoy chanting to myself with my silent whispers (both in the mind and heart) that I am special, I am important, I am loved, I am brilliant, I am powerful, I am at peace. This helps me stay focused on the present and what I am BE-ing. BE-ing/Doing/Having. Leading my life from wherever I am at this point in my life, BE-ing positive, and uplifting myself and as many others as possible.

I have learned one of the best ways to stay positive is to a build my own support system that I can turn to whenever I need support and comfort. Yes, my support system is my family and friends. But most important, it includes my creator (God) and also that one person who is always around everywhere, who knows what I have been through, really knows me the best and will be there until my last breath: my co-creator, which is ME. I like to be the backbone of my own support system, because family and friends are great, but they often are not available in most situations. BE-ing the backbone of my own support system helps me to be the master of creating my life.

Again, coming from the awareness of BE-ing important, I see how really valuable I am. There is only one of me and only one of you in the entire world. I am unique and so are you. Let's cherish and honor ourselves. We are irreplaceable. If we die tomorrow, the world will go on, but our presence will never be replaced. Don't try to be like others; be yourself. Live life enthusiastically, knowing your own specialness! It's only a matter of discovering it in our hearts. Once our specialness is discovered and we can begin to live by it, that will allow others to realize and believe in their own specialness too.

Below is one of my favorite affirmations of specialness from Louise Hay's book *You Can Heal Your Life*:

I love myself, therefore I work from home at a job I truly enjoy doing; one that uses my creative talents and abilities, working with and for people I love and who love me, and earning an amazing income. I love myself, therefore I behave and think in a loving way to all people for I know that which I give out returns to me multiplied. I only attract loving people in my world, for they are a mirror of what I am. I love myself, therefore I forgive and totally release the past and all past experiences, and I am free. I love myself, therefore I live totally in the now, experiencing each moment as good and knowing that my future is bright and joyous and secure, for I am a beloved child of the Universe, and the Universe lovingly takes care of me now and forever more. All is well in my world.

Bringing It All Together with NVC Concepts

I know it is crucial to be open and honest with myself. Lying only creates self-sabotaging behavior to bring me back to being open and honest. Listening and observing more help me become honestly aware of my true feelings and needs. At the same time, by being open and honest, I am able to decrease the evaluations of myself and others and take responsibility for my feelings and needs. I am able to apply the NVC approaches of observing, identifying/ expressing feelings, identifying/expressing needs, and making requests. BE-ing open and honest helps me connect with humanity, because we all have the same human feelings and needs. We just have our own strategies and words for expressing and getting our needs met. Since we share universal feelings and needs, it is important to find the courage to ask questions to clarify and to express what we really want and feel.

Applying Marshall Rosenberg's NVC method helps me connect to my higher true self. I find it to be a true art of communication. For example, Marshall says, "All people ever say is: thank you (a celebration of life) and please (an opportunity to make life more wonderful)." Read his book to discover that meaning.

Using the NVC method gives me the courage to be the leader and the master I was born to be. Remember the courage to be a leader already exists within all of us. All we need to do is to bring awareness to this courage that we were born with, which is rightfully ours.

Though to become a true leader, a master of ourselves, we must first fully love and accept ourselves, then we can understand the wholeness that already exists within us—the wholeness that is achieved for our mind, body, and soul, when we begin operating from our true self. It's all within us. This life is all about US! So, let's communicate nonviolently to ourselves and others.

Recently, I had some unresolved feelings resurface. I was feeling empty inside, as if something was missing in my life. I was feeling sadness and bitterness again. I started to begin aching again. I searched for answers. I discovered I had an old program that was causing such stress. I was amazed after becoming so aware of my programs and patterns that there was more to let go and learn from. The old program I discovered is that in order for me to be happy, everything has to be perfect in my life. How I define perfect changes daily; therefore, perfection seemed impossible to achieve. I was miserable. As I meditated, looking for more answers, I realized I was focusing on the things I did not have in my life. I learned that everything is already perfect. It's just how I perceive it. When I switch to observing versus evaluating, I am able to become aware of the perfection that already exists in all things.

Karol K. Truman explains perfection well in her book *Feelings Buried Alive Never Die*:

> *Whatever the problem, love is the answer. Whatever the fear, love is the answer. Love is all there is. Whatever the question, love is the answer. If we truly love, that love casts out all fear. How does love cast out fear? Real love is unconditional. Real love accepts the perfection of all . . . accepts that EVERYTHING is perfect just the way it is, and EVERYONE is perfect just the way they are! When we accept everything and everyone, the ego doesn't get bogged down with it's fear—fear of not being equal; fear of being rejected; fear of not being good enough; fear of failure; fear of success;*

fear of the future; fear of being unworthy; or whatever the fears may be.

Unconditional love accepts the perfection of all people and all situations just the way they are. This statement can be confusing, because most people want to be better. Too often we look at our incorrectly perceived problems and our incorrect perception of others' faults and we think they are not perfect—that the perfection is to change—that we can't be perfect until we are changed, or someone else is changed. The problem is, too many of us are so emotionally involved in trying to get others to change that we fail to realize that the only person we can really change is numero uno, number one, OURSELF!

There is no reason to feel that you or someone else must change before you can be happy. YOU are the only one you can change . . . and before you can be happy. YOU are the only one you can change . . . and it's necessary to accept yourself despite your shortcomings, before you can change. YOU are the only who can make YOU happy! When we accept ourselves the way we are, we increase our ability to change. And when we start to change, those around us do likewise.

We may still recognize when someone would be happier if they chose to change, but we also understand that it's much easier for us to allow them to change in their own way and at their own speed without our help—as we are not the one responsible for making that change in them. When we arrive at this place in our knowledge and understanding, we naturally move forward in life with more ease. We are more open, more receptive and more able to gain further understanding and knowledge. We are more tolerant and accepting of the experiences that challenge us and teach us those things, which are necessary for our learning and growth. These growth experiences will no longer be a hard procedure we feel we HAVE to go through, but rather one of anticipation that we GET to go through.

The wonderful prospect and attitude of accepting everything and everyone as being perfect is that change is also perfect! What you are going through is perfect. It will cause you to move toward the growth you are to experience, gaining the understanding or learning the lessons that are necessary for you to learn in life.

It all comes back to love. Love is accepting what is. Put another way, unconditional love is understanding, accepting, and letting go of any disagreement or issue.

One of my greatest teachers of all times (F.F.) summed it up for me. He stated either you live in love (coming from love) or you live out of love (are not coming from love). You may go back and forward between being in love and out of love many times a day. The important thing is to realize which state you are in. And if you are out of love, accept your feelings. Usually, if there is any force, threat, or manipulation in your life, you are not coming from love. The choice is yours; you may wish to switch to coming from love. Because LOVE is the only thing that matters. Love is the only truth that exists now and at the end.

In my life journey, I want to be on a path of unconditional love for myself. I am the only one responsible for myself, for what I am thinking, feeling, and doing. I realize my search for true unconditional love and forgiveness for myself will help me operate from a true state of love, respect, peace, and joy. I realize that this true unconditional love and forgiveness already is present within me and within others around me. When I see and feel it, I recognize it because it is often already a part of me and those around me. It's just a matter of discovering it within and then inspiring myself to live in it.

At the same time, I remember the direct connection I have with others and what others have with me:

- When I value myself, I can value others.

- When I love myself, I can love others.

- When I trust myself, I can trust others.

- When I dishonor others, I dishonor myself.

- When I hate others, I hate myself.

A key that helps me live in a state of love is to daily accept and trust the process of life—accepting and trusting that in the end all will be well. Things will work out the way they are supposed to, so I can move on gracefully with my life. That way I am accepting what is and not fighting with what is in my life.

At the same time, I understand that in order for me to have unconditional love and forgiveness for myself and others, it is important for me to accept what the process of life brings my way. Then I can move on, trusting in the process of life that all will be well no matter what happens.

This idea of acceptance was put to the test when I had two deaths in my family. I experienced mixed emotions through the grieving process, going back and forth between sad and happy. When I was feeling happy, I also felt guilty for not feeling sad about my loss. Grieving is a normal part of losing a loved one. But the primary reason I was sad was that I felt sorry for myself, because I wouldn't be seeing my loved ones. I felt sorry for what my family was going through—experiencing so much pain and being left behind to deal with life. After a certain point, even though I wasn't done mourning, I was tired of feeling miserable and wanted to trust in the process and just move on with my life. But it wasn't that easy. My spouse and I had already planned a vacation cruise, and the reservations could not be canceled. I felt guilty for going on vacation while others were grieving. I told myself that while on vacation, I would accept my loss and move on. And in fact, most of the trip went very well. The last day on board the ship, I overheard two men in wheelchairs having a conversation. The first man said to the second, "How could anyone have a terrible time on a cruise ship?" The second man agreed. The first man added, "Unless, of course, you are my wife." Immediately I concluded that the first man's wife must feel sorry for herself, because she is married to a person with a disability.

The next morning I reflected on the man's comments about his wife and on my reaction to them. I wondered why I had so quickly concluded that his wife felt sorry for herself. My evaluation was based on a single comment. I realized then that my conclusion was more about me and my own story. It was not about the man and his wife but about my own struggles.

It's interesting how discovering myself is an ongoing process. Every time I think I understand it, there is more to learn. Discovering the self and the programs and patterns is a process like cutting through an onion and seeing all the different layers. My experience hearing the man on the ship helped me discover another hidden program. I was surprised to see how I was going through life feeling sorry for myself. From the outside I appeared to be a very balanced person but inside, I was very different. The more I brought my awareness to this belief the more I realized I was carrying a deep sorrow. I reflected on the situations where I had felt this sorrow for myself. In most cases it was when I considered I had missed opportunities in my life. I felt sorry for what I didn't experience, for what I didn't have. I hid from my feelings for so long. At the surface I was a very grateful person, but my inner experience was different.

As you see, I am constantly discovering, accepting, and moving forward. I support myself by forgiving myself and providing myself with unconditional love. I read affirmations such, "I live without judging myself. I know what it feels to love myself unconditionally. I am enough."

Below are thoughts from my favorite spiritual teachers of all times:

I read Rumi's poem to remind myself of how very special I am and how very special everyone around me really is.

i swear my dear son

no one in the entire world

is as precious as you are

look at that mirror

take a good look at yourself

who else is there above and beyond you?

now give yourself a kiss

and with sweet whispers

fill your ears to the brim

watch for all that beauty

reflecting from you and sing a love song to your existence

you can never overdo

praising your own soul

you can never over-pamper your heart

you are both

the father and the son

the mother and the daughter

the sugar and the sugar cane

who else but you

please tell me who else

can ever take your place

now give yourself a smile

what is the worth of a diamond

if it doesn't shine

how can i ever put a price

on the diamond that you are

you are the entire treasure of the house

you and your shadow

are forever present in this world

you're that glorious bird of paradise.

Brendon Burchard, "I feel alive today because today is a blessing. In this moment, I can find misery or meaning, boredom or motivation. I can expand the hatred in the world, or I can amplify love. In all the chaos, I can find stillness and joy within. All is well, and nothing has to happen to "give" me more happiness in life. I simply choose to be happy now, to be grateful now, to be a source of love and light for others. I am whole. I am ready. This is my day."

Robert Holden,

"Self-love is not about vanity or arrogance, it's about self-respect...it's a deep appreciation for how you've been made and for the life you are here to live. The more we love ourselves, the less we project our pain onto the world. When we stop judging ourselves, we naturally judge others less. When we stop attacking ourselves, we naturally judge others less. When we stop rejecting ourselves, we stop accusing others of hurting us. When we start loving ourselves more, we become happier, less defended, and more open. As we love ourselves, we naturally love others more. Self-love is the greatest gift because what you give yourself is experienced by others.

Wayne Dryer,

If you change the way you look at things, the things you look at change.
How people treat you is their karma; how you react is yours.
When you judge another, you do not define them, you define yourself.

When you acquire enough inner peace and feel really positive about yourself, it's almost impossible for you to be controlled and manipulated by anyone else.

Special Thanks

I want to give special thanks and honor to my dear parents, whom I love and adore. They have given me so much of their time, energy, and love that I am ever so grateful to them. They are also the best teachers I could ever have wished for. Because of them, I am here and well today.

At first, my mother gave me so much love, compassion, and tenderness that I don't have words to fully describe them. She is one of the gentlest and wisest women I have ever met. My mother is a brilliant woman! She has provided me emotional, physical, and spiritual support throughout my life. Her teachings of seeing the good in all and staying positive are a part of my body, mind, and soul.

My father worked three jobs to support us. He was the sole provider for my mom, my siblings, and me. I realize how hard he strives to provide for us. He is really a magnificent man! Also, I am grateful to him for introducing me to and providing direction in religion, teaching me rituals and practices that I still follow today. His philosophy has become the backbone of who I am today. Just recently he reminded me to keep my heart clear of hate, envy, and jealousy. The heart is meant to Love.

Both of my parents are true gems. I really value and appreciate everything they have done for me because I know they did the best they could to raise me and provide for me. That is all any person can do in life—to do their best with what they have been given, and to forgive and love.

Also, special thanks to my spouse for loving, supporting, and believing in me. You have mirrored me well, which has helped me continue to grow. Your encouragement means a whole lot and you mean everything to me. I love you!

Very loving thanks to my three incredible children for being present in my life and for just being themselves. You all are so very special, and I love you very much. I am so honored to co-parent you.

There are so many more people like my siblings, aunts, uncles, cousins, other relatives, friends, and who have touched my life in such a special way. I am forever grateful to all of you; to all of my teachers known and unknown. List continues endlessly with much appreciation.

A very special thanks to all who have helped me make this book possible!

Favorite Quotes:
Our ultimate freedom is the right and power to decide how anybody or anything outside ourselves will affect us.

~ Stephen R. Covey ~

I think perfectionism is based on the obsessive belief that if you run carefully enough, hitting each stepping-stone just right, you won't have to die. The truth is you will die anyway and that a lot of people who aren't even looking at their feet are going to do a whole lot better than you, and have a lot more fun while they're doing it.

~ Anne Lamott ~

"*It's choice—not chance—that determines your destiny.*"

~ Jean Nidetch ~

High five forever!

~ Vibrant 7-year-old ~

> *Accept—then act. Whatever the present moment contains, accept it as if you had chosen it. Always work with it, not against it.*
> *~ Eckhart Tolle ~*

There are two ways of exerting one's strength: one is pushing down, the other is pulling up.

~ Booker T. Washington ~

"Believe Big. The size of your success is determined by the size of your belief. Think little goals and expect little achievements. Think big goals and win big success. Remember this, too! Big ideas and big plans are often easier—certainly no more difficult—than small ideas and small plans."

~ David J. Scwartz ~

Make the present good, and the past will take care of itself.

~ Knute Rockne ~

You wake up in the morning, and your purse is magically filled with twenty-four hours of unmanufactured tissue of the universe of your life! It is yours. It is the most precious of possessions. No one can take it from you. And no one receives either more or less than you receive.

~ Dr. Thomas Arnold Bennett ~

Men often become what they believe themselves to be. If I believe I cannot do something, it makes me incapable of doing it. But when I believe I can, then I acquire the ability to do it even if I didn't have it in the beginning.
  ~ Mahatma Gandhi ~

Kindness in words creates confidence.
Kindness in thinking creates profoundness.
Kindness in giving creates love.
  ~ Lao Tzu ~

At the center of your being you have the answer; you know who you are and you know what you want.
~ Lao Tzu ~

Be Content with what you have; rejoice in the way things are. When you realize there is nothing lacking, the whole world belongs to you.
~ Lao Tzu ~

Be the chief but never the lord.
~ Lao Tzu ~

Knowing others is wisdom, knowing yourself is Enlightenment.
~ Lao Tzu ~

Life and death are one thread, the same line viewed from different sides.
~ Lao Tzu ~

"I am fundamentally an optimist. Whether that comes from nature or nurture. I cannot say. Part of being optimistic is keeping one's head pointed toward the sun, one's feet moving forward. There were many dark moments when my faith in humanity was sorely tested, but I would not and could not give myself up to despair…..I learned that courage was not the absence of fear, but the triumph over it. The brave man is not he who does not feel afraid, but he who conquers fear." – Nelson Mandela

"Even

After

All this time

The Sun never says

To the Earth,

"you owe me".

Look

What happens

With a love like that.

It lights the

Whole Sky"   **Poet Hafiz**

References:

Marshall Rosenberg's, *Nonviolent Communication: Language of Life*

Inbal Kashtan, *Parenting From Your Heart*

Sura Hart and Victoria Kindle Hodson, *Respectful Parents, Respectful Kids*

Personal Success Institute Basic Seminar, PSI

David Simon, *Free to Love, Free to Heal*

Karol K. Truman, *Feelings Buried Alive Never Die.*

Vitalaffirmations.com

Louise Hay's book, *You Can Heal Your Life*

John-Roger and Paul Kaye, *The Rest of Your Life: Finding Repose in the Beloved*

Denise Malayeri

Hakim Archuletta,

Marianne Williamson

www.ingramcontent.com/pod-product-compliance
Lightning Source LLC
Chambersburg PA
CBHW071736080526
44588CB00013B/2048